ARCHAEOLOGY

John Manley

First published in Great Britain in 2014 by Hodder and Stoughton. An Hachette UK company.

First published in US in 2014 by The McGraw-Hill Companies, Inc.

This edition published 2014

Copyright © John Manley 2014

British Library Cataloguing in Publication Data: a catalogue record for this title is available from the British Library.

Library of Congress Catalog Card Number: on file.

Paperback ISBNL 9781471801594

Ebook ISBN: 9781471805639

10 9 8 7 6 5 4 3 2 1

Typeset by Cenveo® Publisher Services.

Printed and bound in Great Britain by CPI Group (UK) Ltd., Croydon, CR0 4YY.

John Murray Learning policy is to use papers that are natural, renewable and recyclable products and made from wood grown in sustainable forests. The logging and manufacturing processes are expected to conform to the environmental regulations of the country of origin.

John Murray Learning

338 Euston Road

London NW1 3BH

www.hodder.co.uk

Contents

Photo credits

Introduction Sussex kitchen window-ledge © John Manley.
Chapter 1 Augustus Henry Lane-Fox Pitt Rivers © Pictorial Press Ltd /
Alamy. **Chapter 2** Crop-Mark © Clwyd-Powys Archaeological Trust.
Chapter 3 Silchester Excavations by the University of Reading © John
Manley. **Chapter 4** An archaeologist using an EDM © Pool DEVILLE/
AFSM/Gamma-Rapho via Getty Images. **Chapter 5** Recording
pottery sherds © Luke Barber. **Chapter 6** A Kenyah Hunter. © Royal
Anthropological Institute 11023. From an album of photographs
by Charles Hose, c. 1884–1926. **Chapter 7** Kgatla Women © Royal
Anthropological Institute 3988. Kgatla women threshing corn.
Photograph by Isaac Schapera, c. 1920-30. **Chapter 8** Son of a Samoan
Chief © Royal Anthropological Institute 10746. From the J.P. Mills
collection (photgrapher unknown). **Chapter 9** Arch of Titus © John
Manley. **Chapter 10** A Nkisi By kind permission of Mark P. Leone as
Director of Archaeology in Annapolis; The East Side Gallery, Berlin
© Tim Johnson; Gobëkli Tepe, Turkey © Vincent J. Musi/National
Geographic Society/Corbis.

Introduction

Archaeological discoveries are by their very nature often unpredictable. They also come in many different guises. In September 2010 the photographer Rä di Martino spent a month travelling around the Chott el Djerid, the great salt desert in Tunisia, looking for a particular type of archaeological site – not deserted Roman settlements or Islamic towns but abandoned Hollywood and European film sets. All successful archaeological projects need a bit of luck. And some friendly locals. She got both. In the end Rä located three sets from *Star Wars*, including the decaying remains of Luke Skywalker's childhood home. For her these modern ruins had a monumentality about them because they resonated with her own childhood memories. She eventually published the pictures. *Star Wars* enthusiasts were saddened by the state of the site, but ultimately determined to do something about it. Over $11,000 was raised and some of the fans spent four days working with locals restoring Luke's original domicile.

Many of us, especially those who live in the more affluent countries of the world, have a rough idea of what archaeologists do, although perhaps not many would have included a *Stars Wars* set in their list of heritage sites to visit. We have seen archaeologists on our televisions, tablets or laptops. We have strolled through museums, or wandered around archaeological sites on holiday, or even visited an excavation. They are the people who dig holes in the ground, uncovering buildings and tombs, pieces of flint, pottery or metalwork. They analyse them, and then tell us enthusiastically what it all means. We watch appreciatively, marvelling at their excitement while simultaneously wondering why they don't look more like Indiana Jones or Lara Croft. We are perplexed by what all those people in that hole or trench are doing. How do they know where and what to dig, and whether to dig quickly or carefully? We do not necessarily understand the entire significance of their discoveries, but we appreciate that some small part of our knowledge of the past is being amplified before our eyes.

One question that we could think about – but often don't – is why people do archaeology at all? Perhaps this is seldom asked because the whole business of archaeology – wanting to know about things that you find in the ground – taps into a natural curiosity and seems second-nature. Let me give you an example. You are digging in a garden – and your spade turns up part of a bottle, or the rim of plate. Grateful of any pretext to put down your spade, you pick up the artefact, brush the dirt off and examine its shape. You might begin to wonder how your fragment fitted into the complete object, whether plate or bottle. What did it once contain or hold? How, and where, was it made? How did it get to the bottom of your garden? Who owned it? And where is the rest of it? Once you start asking these questions you become less of a gardener, and more of an archaeologist. You might just throw the piece back into the soil and continue digging. But you might put the sherd in your pocket, wash it when you get back in the house, put it on the kitchen window ledge to dry. A curiosity! You are still a gardener – but you have taken the first step towards becoming an archaeologist.

▲ Some people begin to get curious about the past by finding something in the garden. On my Sussex kitchen window-ledge a prize exhibit is the base of an old wine bottle.

Another question, this time more frequently asked, is how things, ranging from small bits of pottery to whole cities, get buried in the first place. There are some obvious answers. If you had farmed in the countryside around Pompeii and Herculaneum in 79 CE you would have witnessed the eruption of Vesuvius, cursing the gods as falling pumice stones and pyroclastic flows buried entire cities in the matter of a few days. Some settlements are buried rather more slowly, such as those in valleys or at the base of slopes that are gradually covered in layers of soil eroding from higher ground. In long-lived urban sites, redundant buildings are levelled, rubbish accumulates, and new structures are erected on old.

My favourite example of this process of 'covering up' returns us to the garden and to the humble worm. A famous Professor of Archaeology, now long dead, once remarked that the body mass of all the worms under a field of grass could easily equate to the body mass of cattle grazing that grass. Now worms, despite having no teeth, digest and aerate soil, often leaving casts of digested soil on the surface. Do this experiment. Place a small sheet of metal on your lawn. Come back fifty years later. Hungry worms should have done their job. Your metal will have sunk a little, and become buried with upcast soil – plus all the other organic matter that will have accumulated in the meantime. Fifty years is a long time to wait, so you might have to take my word on this one!

Archaeology is not that difficult. Bear with me for one final garden example. String out a square, one metre a side. Keeping the sides as vertical as you can, dig down in horizontal layers, each of say 100 millimetres. Call the first layer 1, the second one down layer 2, and so on. If you are lucky you probably will find one or two small manufactured things – bits of brick, glass, pottery, the odd nail. Put them in a bag and write the number of the layer they come from on the bag. Stop when you get below the soil level. In my garden I would get through about three layers before I hit what some archaeologists call 'the natural' – deposits laid down by geological processes a long time before human beings were around – that is a solid clay in my case. Now, assuming your garden has not been subjected to too much disturbance in the past, the objects you find in your bottom-most layer should be the oldest, while those at the top should be the youngest. That's the theory anyway. Congratulations! You have just completed your first dig!

Lastly, how do you become an archaeologist? Most professional archaeologists, those who are lucky enough to get paid to do it, have studied the subject to degree-level and found a position in a museum, a university or a central or local government agency. Some are employed by commercial organizations that generate their income from construction companies wanting to build houses or roads, or open quarries. In some countries planning legislation requires that developers must pay for archaeological survey and excavation, if necessary in advance of such developments. But some archaeologists are not paid, nor do they possess academic qualifications. These are people who volunteer on 'digs'. A few gain considerable experience and even carry out their own excavations, usually for local community groups or societies.

It really brings the village together. You get to meet new people and it's a great experience. We have learnt so much in such a short time.

VR, a Willingham (UK) resident on Willingham Village Community Dig

You don't have to have any previous knowledge or skill-set to get involved at a novice level, as a volunteer. Indeed, if you join a local archaeological group or society you will bring to any dig your own, unique, perspective on 'what it all means'.

This book is an introduction to archaeology and I have structured it in a particular way. After an opening chapter that examines the origins of archaeology, there are four chapters that describe in outline the processes of developing, undertaking and publishing an archaeological project. The next four chapters explore how archaeologists use the monuments and artefacts they dig up to speculate on the sorts of communities who built those monuments or fashioned those artefacts – hunters and gatherers or farmers, chiefdoms or states. I am a firm believer that archaeologists should always seek to infer from the things they find the kinds of society that produced them. It's not the pots that are important, but what people did with the pots! I finish off with a chapter on the role of archaeology in the historical and modern periods.

Note that in this book I have used the abbreviation BCE for Before the Common/Current/Christian Era and CE for the Common/Current/Christian Era as alternatives to Before Christ (BC) and Anno Domini (AD).

1

Archaeology in the beginning ...

Now that's sad, because after all, archaeology is fun. Hell, I don't break the soil periodically to 'reaffirm my status'. I do it because archaeology is still the most fun you can have with your pants on.

Kent V. Flannery, 1982

The story begins, not in Europe, the Far East or the New World, but in Africa. It seems quite likely that *Homo sapiens* – the species you and I belong to – emerged in Africa some 200,000 years ago gradually spreading to all habitable locations on the planet. Our bigger brains gave us language, the ability to make tools, walk upright, light fires, cook food and clothe ourselves and, crucially, a facility for imagination and abstract reasoning.

When it comes to thinking about the past it seems plausible that many ancient communities, when confronted with artefacts that seemed different or putatively older than themselves, were naturally curious about them. There are a number of examples: a Balkan princess of the 5th century BCE had a collection of much older stone axes in her grave; native American sites of the 15th and 16th centuries CE sometimes contain objects made a thousand years earlier; Roman graves occasionally contain prehistoric stone axes. This curiosity about ancient objects was not stirred by a desire to discover 'objective' facts; much more likely is the possibility that some kind of magical agency had been accorded these items, perhaps protective powers, and hence their discovery in graves – where the deceased, or their surviving relatives, presumably hoped that such powers could protect in the afterlife as well.

▶ Early archaeology

If we want to pin down the first archaeological excavation, then there are two possible candidates. The earliest was during New Kingdom Egypt (1550–1070 BCE), when the Pharaohs excavated and reconstructed the

Sphinx, built during the 4th Dynasty (Old Kingdom, 2575–2134 BCE) for the Pharaoh Khafre. There are no written records to support the excavation, but physical evidence of the reconstruction exists, and there are ivory carvings from earlier periods that indicate the Sphinx was buried in sand up to its head and shoulders before the New Kingdom excavations. The second candidate is Nabonidus, king of Babylon, who in the 6th century BCE excavated a temple floor to reveal a foundation stone of a much earlier building.

The Romans, as might be expected, displayed a variety of attitudes to the past, some quite familiar to us today. The soldiers of Julius Caesar, founding and settling in colonies in Italy and Greece, robbed many ancient tombs for their pottery and bronzes, knowing that they would fetch a high price amongst the collectors in Rome. Clearly this was an early example of the trade in antiquities. The emperors, and the elite, valued antiquities for their cultural rather than monetary value. The first emperor, Augustus, was a noted collector of foreign coins, while one of his successors, Hadrian, decked out his villa at Tivoli with Greek and Egyptian art-works. In the 2nd century CE the Greek temple of Zeus at Olympia possessed numerous bronzes and statues, including bronze horses from a 5th-century BCE King of Sparta and statues of Trajan and Hadrian – a group of objects not out of place in a late-Renaissance collection.

Most of the medieval period was characterized by superstitious beliefs about ancient artefacts, and often they were not recognized as made by humans at all, but believed to be the work of gods, or magical creatures like elves and witches. The surface of the ground was always being disturbed somewhere, by new building, erosion, mining, ploughing or the burrowing of animals, and buried objects occasionally made their way to the surface. In various places around the world they were collected, and, if small in size frequently venerated as charms, sometimes being perforated and hung around the neck.

▶ Archaeology in the Renaissance

No doubt these attitudes to ancient objects continued for many centuries, but notions among the European elite were gradually changed by their involvement with the Renaissance. This broad movement, from the 14th to the 17th centuries CE, affected the countries of Europe in different ways, but common themes included an emphasis on learning through recovery and translation of classical Greek and Roman texts, and architectural movements that sprang from the study of classical antiquities, particularly the ancient buildings of Rome itself. As wealthy individuals collected sculpture and pottery vases for their palatial homes, a gradual awareness dawned of the antiquity of more mundane objects and of surviving earthworks much closer to home. So much so that some very rich patrons took to gathering together a variety of archaeological, geological, religious and natural history specimens and presenting them in a so-called 'cabinet of curiosities'. Whatever their motivation, these private cabinets were the first museum displays.

▶ Setting the standards for modern archaeology

The late 18th and first half of the 19th centuries constituted a crucial period for the development of archaeology as an embryonic academic discipline. Knowledge about the origins of humankind up to that point, in the Western world at least, had been shackled by Christian teaching to a problematically precise chronology. It was James Ussher (1581–1656), the famous and respected Archbishop of Armagh and Primate of All Ireland, who had calculated from the Book of Genesis that humans were created in October 4004 BCE.

> I deduce that the time from the creation until midnight, January 1, 1 AD was 4003 years, seventy days and six hours.
>
> *Bishop Ussher*

Increasingly the evidence from archaeological discoveries began to put pressure on such a constrained timeframe. The pivotal discovery was made by a French customs inspector, Jacques Boucher de Perthes. He explored the gravel quarries near the Somme River in northern France, and in 1841 published convincing evidence of the association of flint artefacts (hand-axes) with the bones of extinct animals. He argued successfully that this demonstrated the presence of human beings a long time before the supposed biblical flood. Others agreed and the possibility of a pre-biblical, prehistoric period for human existence gradually became an accepted certainty.

The techniques of excavation were also being established at this time. Thomas Jefferson (1743–1826), later to become the third President of the United States, dug a trench across a burial mound on his property in Virginia in 1784. People were speculating at the time that hundreds of unexplained mounds east of the Mississippi could not have been built by Native Americans but by a mythical and vanished race of Moundbuilders. Jefferson tested this hypothesis by making accurate observations of the different layers in the mound, and by noting the quantity and state of preservation of human bones in each layer. He argued that the mound could have been repeatedly used for burials on many occasions, and that he saw no reason why the mound could not have been built by Native Americans.

Two other major intellectual advances provided the springboard for the birth of archaeology proper. In 1836 the Danish scholar C.J. Thomsen published a guidebook to the National Museum of Copenhagen. It was to prove one of the most influential guidebooks of all time. He proposed that his collections could be chronologically ordered into a succession of 'Ages' – a Stone Age, then a Bronze Age and lastly an Iron Age. Although not applicable throughout the world, Thomsen had demonstrated that by studying and classifying ancient objects you could produce a chronological ordering. Such classificatory ordering was also apparent in museum displays of other types of collection. Ethnographic objects, most collected by colonial officials and missionaries from exotic locations in places like Africa or the South Pacific, were organized too by this paradigm, with the simplest or most 'primitive' at the bottom of the hierarchy and the most complex or 'civilized' at the top. A second seismic shift came with the publication of Darwin's *On the Origins of Species* in 1859, which argued that the evolution of plants and animals occurred through natural selection or the survival of the fittest. The implications were that the human species must have evolved by similar mechanisms. Archaeology was the obvious tool with which to investigate this further.

Interest in archaeology among the general public really took off in the latter half of the 19th century. The wonders of ancient Egypt had already attracted significant attention as a result of Napoleon's expedition there of 1798–1801. Western 'tourists' flooded into Egypt after 1815 including an American lawyer and diplomat, John Lloyd Stephens (1805–1852), who then travelled to the Yucatán together with an English artist, Francis Catherwood, whom he met in the Near East. They produced superbly illustrated books in the 1840s revealing for the first time the dramatically ruinous cities of the ancient Maya. Later in the century, inspired by Homer's *Iliad*, a German banker, Heinrich Schliemann, discovered the remains of Troy in western Turkey and then went on to reveal a previously unrecognized Bronze Age civilization at Mycenae, in Greece. These early excavations were often conducted on a large scale but with minimal attention to the details of stratigraphy (the successive layers or deposits on a site) or any great accuracy in recording methods. They were a product of their time and it was to fall to the next generation of archaeologists to establish more rigorous methodologies for fieldwork.

Early pioneers

General Pitt Rivers (1827–1900) was, for much of his life, a professional soldier, and he brought military standards of precise survey to archaeological fieldwork. On his estate at Cranborne Chase in southern England, he excavated prehistoric burial mounds and recorded his work with commendable detail. He drew plans and sections (of vertical profiles) as his trenches became gradually deeper. His methods of recovery were truly pioneering and he insisted on recording the positions of every single object he came across, no matter how mundane. Never again would archaeology be just about retrieving beautiful treasures from the ground. At the end of his life he published all his results in four volumes setting the standards for archaeological publication for years to come.

That insistence on meticulous recording of every object found on an excavation was carried on by Flinders Petrie (1853–1942) in Egypt and Palestine. In particular Petrie was credited with the invention of seriation or sequence-dating, bringing chronological order to some 2200 pit graves he had excavated at Naqada in Upper Egypt. First the grave-goods in each grave were catalogued in detail, then similar graves were grouped together, adjacent to others that were only marginally different, until a complete sequence of all the graves was produced. In this fashion subtle and gradual changes amongst the grave-goods could be observed running through the entire chronological order.

Mortimer Wheeler (1890–1976), another former British soldier, also brought a military orderliness to the techniques of excavation, assisted immeasurably by his wife, Tessa. He famously invented the grid-square method, by which sites were examined through a lattice of excavated squares, separated from each other by un-excavated earthen baulks.

His administrative skills came to the fore in India, where, as Director-General of Archaeology, he laid the basis for modern investigative methods on the sub-continent. On the other side of the Atlantic figures like Alfred Kidder (1885–1963) revolutionized the analysis of finds by recruiting a team of specialists to study artefacts and human remains in the American South-west. He also developed new methodologies for surveying and subsequently investigating archaeological sites over a large region.

▲ Augustus Henry Lane-Fox Pitt Rivers (1827–1900) was an English army officer and archaeologist. He improved the precision of archaeological excavation by introducing more rigorous recording methods. His many excavations included one at the great hillfort of Cissbury Ring, near Worthing, in southern England.

> There is no right way of digging, but there are many wrong ways.
>
> *Mortimer Wheeler*

▶ Modern approaches to archaeology

The pace of archaeological discoveries and new techniques of investigation in the 20th century increased, alongside a growing public awareness and appreciation of the past. If there is one particular invention that was utterly transformative for understanding the chronologies of ancient communities it was that announced by the American Willard Libby in 1949 – the discovery that organic materials such as charcoal recovered on archaeological sites could be dated by measuring their amount of the Carbon-14 isotope. This paved the way for archaeologists to date sites, or layers in their sites, independently from artefacts found in association with them.

The broad philosophy underlying archaeological interpretation also went through some major conceptual shifts during the 20th century. In the first fifty years or so prehistoric sites in particular regions were grouped together by similarities in terms of site morphology or artefacts, and described as belonging to the same 'culture' or society. Changes in objects or sites over time were described loosely as the result of one culture 'influencing' another, or by population movement. The overall interpretative framework was a descriptive one. All that was to change with the advent of *The New Archaeology* in the 1960s. An influential American archaeologist, Lewis Binford, was the flag-bearer for a brave, new archaeological manifesto. The emphasis was to be on quasi-scientific approach to excavation. Archaeologists should first draw up hypotheses and then test them through fieldwork. The focus was not on description but on explicit explanation of past change, using quantitative methods. This approach to the study of the past came to be known by archaeologists as *processual*.

A reaction to this *scientistic* approach emerged in the closing decades of the 20th century with the rise of a *post-processual* archaeology. Here the proposition that 'truths' about the past could be revealed by quantitative approaches was rejected. Instead, through much borrowing of ideas from sister disciplines such as social or cultural anthropology and sociology, new interpretative insights were applied to excavated buildings and objects. Entire landscapes, buildings and artefacts were seen as imbued with symbolic meaning, all of which could influence the communities who lived with them. Such meanings would never be recovered by reducing everything to numbers.

Finally the scepticism of post-modernism and the hindsight of post-colonial movements belatedly affected archaeological interpretation. From these particular vantage points interpretation of the past was democratized. It was no longer appropriate for the archaeological elite of developed countries to provide the only authoritative voice on the past. Indigenous leaders and communities had an equally valid perspective on their history; perhaps more so. In addition archaeologists eventually recognized that there was no such thing as an 'objective truth' about the past, and that the interpretations they imagined were not real reconstructions of the past as it was, but the past as they imagined it to be. Indeed, they needed to reflect on their own particular biases, and own up to them, if the results of their fieldwork could be properly evaluated by others. There was no universal archaeological methodology. Researchers had for a long time noted that archaeological methodologies and emphases differed from country to country.

The discipline of archaeology has come a long, unpredictable way in the last 200 years. It will continue to develop its own trajectory. But for the time being we must pause and get back to basics with some obvious questions. Before a spade or trowel disturbs the ground, just where do archaeologists get their ideas from about what to look for – and where to look for it?

2

Before you dig ...

Conducting archaeological research is a privilege, not a right.

Al Tonetti, ASC Group, Inc.

The days are long gone when archaeologists could just select, almost at random, an interesting settlement, or cave, or burial mound, and excavate a few trenches just to 'see what was there'. Things are, quite rightly, a lot more organized and controlled now. To start with, archaeologists usually have quite specific interests, and skills and knowledge to go with them. They can specialize in a particular country and/or in a specific period of the past, or a type of a site. So you might get one person who is interested in indigenous ritual sites in West Africa, or a Roman archaeologist who specializes in military sites in the Eastern Roman Empire. These people are knowledgeable in their field and know what information is currently lacking. The African scholar might want to know more about how local objects were used in rituals, and whether the encroachment of western European colonialism affected those artefacts. The Romanist might want to discover more about the late Roman fortifications in Syria, and the strategic thinking behind them.

▶ The research design

You can see from this how the germ of an idea for an archaeological project begins with a series of questions. However, turning these questions into the reality of a proper field campaign of excavations and surveys is a challenging process, especially if the project is a salvage one, where time is at a premium. However time-pressured they are, most archaeologists start with the notion of a written *Research Design*; indeed, in some countries, if the project is to be accepted and funded, a well-argued

Research Design is essential. These documents are not things that can be dashed off in a matter of days or weeks. One excavator of famous Saxon burial mounds at Sutton Hoo, in eastern England, asked his funders for no fewer than three years to come up with a Research Design. So what should one of these crucial documents contain?

First you need the *formulation of a research strategy* to resolve a particular archaeological and historical question, or to test specific hypotheses or ideas. One of the important things here is that the strategy has to be practical. It might be fascinating to know more about the cargoes of sunken Spanish Armada ships off the coasts of the British Isles, but the waters that conceal them may be too deep, murky or dangerous. And it would be really interesting to learn more about Native Australian beliefs by excavating caves near Uluru in central Australia, but indigenous elders may be wholly opposed to the disturbance of ancestral sites by such investigations. So practicality, within a specified time frame, are two of the key parameters.

Then you need a clear proposal for *pre-fieldwork assessment*, involving library research, scrutiny of archives and extant air photographs, examination of previous fieldwork in the area and perusal of historic maps. Essentially you are promising to review everything there is to know about a particular area and subject before you plan a campaign of fieldwork proper. Next comes *fieldwork strategy* itself. This can be broken down into two components. The first is a series of proposed non-intrusive steps (i.e. no actual digging) which can involve new aerial photography, field-walking to collect surface artefacts and various remote-sensing methods such as resistivity or magnetometry. Second will come the actual excavation of trenches to test hypotheses laid out in the original research strategy. An important element of the *fieldwork strategy* is the personnel. Just how many people do you need? Where are you going to recruit them? What skills should they have? And, just as important, where are they going to stay? An additional people factor is the involvement of the local communities. How are these people going to be integrated into your project? What are their opinions?

The subsequent element in the Research Design is a section on *processing and analysis*. How are all the different categories of finds and features – from, for example, flint flakes, pottery sherds, animal bones, seeds and charcoals, to pits, post holes, ditches, walls and buildings – going to be analysed? Who is going to carry out these analyses, with what methods and at what cost, and again, over what time-frame? Which categories of evidence are more likely to answer some of the questions you posed in the research strategy?

The final component of a Research Design is the one relating to the dissemination of the results – *publication* – again within a reasonable time-frame. Some archaeologists, unfortunately, find this last major element quite tedious. Part of the problem is psychological. Any excavator will tell you that there is a certain buzz about archaeological fieldwork. It is exciting to dream up research ideas, to be fired with enthusiasm coming up with some new insights into this or that problem. It is even more exhilarating to be out in the field, surrounded by a small army of co-workers, undertaking surveys, or excavating trenches. The discoveries don't come as thick and fast as they do on television documentaries, but they do come – and there is the thrill of being the first to find this, and to prove that.

However, then comes the long post-excavation process of getting the results written up. This is a very different sort of archaeological work from the fieldwork. It is usually a solitary task, carried out by the excavation director. The provisional results have been known for some time, but may be altered as more definitive information arises from post-excavation work. The final exposition in prose, presenting all the evidence for the new interpretations, and the answers to some of those ideas laid out in the research strategy, takes time, often years, and sadly, in some cases, more than life-times. Archaeologists are only human, and sometimes the itch to get out in the field again overwhelms the feeling of duty to remain in the study until publication of the last fieldwork is complete. Moreover, publication nowadays takes many forms – the online blog during the dig, the interim report for funders and colleagues, the popular publication for the general public, the scholarly report for posterity, and the digital archive of dig records.

▶ Gathering the first data

Well, the Research Design is done, dusted, and, what's more significant, funded. Armed with the document you now have to deliver what it promises. Passionate is an inappropriate term to apply to most archaeologists, but some of them feel suitably wide-eyed and inspired at the start of projects. First comes the comprehensive trawl through all potential sources that can tell you something about the development of a region or a site in the past. This will involve reading about any previous descriptive works or archaeological work in the area – from accounts by early explorers centuries ago, to published (or unpublished) records from previous excavations. Depending on where you are in the world there may be institutions that maintain summary archaeological records of all sites in a region – such as those maintained by the National Parks Service in the United States or the Historic Environment Records of Local Authorities in England. There may also be museums that contain unpublished collections of artefacts from your intended study area.

Most importantly, do not overlook the contributions of local people. It is unlikely that, for instance, local farm-workers on Salisbury Plain would be able to tell you much about what Stonehenge was originally used for. But on the other hand they might well know about a curious concentration of flints in one part of a field, or the presence of a slight mound hidden in an out-of-the-way copse – small but potentially significant clues.

Caution!

Documentary evidence needs to be assessed with caution. Just because a 15th-century document does not mention any settlements in a particular region does not necessarily mean that there were none. The perspective of the recorder must always be considered. The observer may have encountered local settlements that were so different from what was expected that they were not recorded as such. Secondly very old documents often come down to us second or third hand. For example, the *Journal of Christopher Columbus*, which comments on prehistoric people encountered in the Caribbean, is an abstract made by a Dominican historian from a lost copy drafted by two scribes. In a similar vein, ancient Roman historians often used information copied from earlier historians whose works do not now survive. In Europe, medieval records may enumerate in great detail expenditure on a royal castle, but neglect a peasant farmstead just outside its walls. These types of documents hardly ever describe objectively, but instead comment for a specific purpose on what was deemed to be important.

Maps are a vital source but must be used critically. Until the 18th century most of them tended to be pictorial rather than cartographically accurate. Thus a 1657 map of Barbados shows schematic pictures of houses more or less regularly spaced around the coast, in the right order by land-owner. However, it is a thankless task trying to locate precisely any of these properties on the ground, just from the details provided by the map.

Another significant group of techniques deployed before any ground is disturbed fall collectively under the term *remote sensing*. This simply means using a method to try and assess what is beneath the ground remotely, without penetrating it physically. The principal elements comprise satellite images, aerial photography and geophysics. The availability of Google Earth and other satellite photography has allowed every armchair archaeologist in the world the opportunity to look for new trackways and sites. In 2008 detailed examination of imagery from Google Earth facilitated the discovery of 500 new caves in South Africa, while hundreds of settlements and sites were found by this method in Afghanistan, and elsewhere in the Near East.

▲ The main pattern of dark marks in this field is formed by less ripe corn probably growing over ditches surrounding an Iron Age or Romano-British farm in Wales.

Aerial photography has had an important role in archaeological detection for a long time. Undiscovered sites reveal themselves by causing differential growth patterns in cereals (hence the name crop mark) or soils. In the case of the former, for instance, crops will grow taller over a filled-in ditch, and be stunted lying over the masonry footings of a wall. LiDAR (Light Detection and Ranging) is another technique of aerial surveillance. A laser scanner pulses beams to the ground and the time taken for these to return is converted into a digital surface model. This method is especially useful in wooded areas, such as the forests of Belize. Hundreds of new features have been revealed through LiDAR associated with the Mayan city of Caracol. It takes skill and experience to find and interpret sites through satellite or aerial photography. A famous US astronomer's quote is highly relevant here:

> Absence of Evidence is not Evidence of Absence.
>
> *Carl Sagan*

The final element of remote sensing is a battery of geophysical techniques, such as resistivity, magnetometry and ground-penetrating radar. The first works on mapping electrical resistances in the ground, the second on mapping magnetic variations and the third by mapping reflections of radio pulses. Often excavators utilize all three methods, since one method will work better on different areas of a site than others. To be honest, the excitement of these techniques all comes at the end, when in the 'reveal' moment, the computer spews out a pattern of light and dark that just might be meaningful. If it looks like a rectangular or circular building, or a square grave-pit then 'Eureka!' But more often than not it's an indeterminate smudge that just might be something. The hard slog of capturing the data is made a lot easier these days through wheeled resistivity meters, data loggers and specialized software to crunch and pattern the numbers.

▶ Surface survey

The final component before you start excavating is a *surface survey* and collection (or observation) of surface material. The latter most often takes the form of pottery fragments (or sherds) or flint scatters. Occasionally other surface debris might be present such as shells (from buried shell refuse or middens), scatters of stones or patches of differently coloured soil. There is a substantial body of literature on sampling methods to use in your surveys, since, especially if your target region is large, you won't be able to walk across every open space – you will only be able to cover a fraction of the area. In addition, there may be some pockets of land that you cannot survey, such as underneath modern roads or shopping malls, or militarized areas that are off-limits. But the point about sampling theory is that you are supposed to be able to extrapolate your findings from a small percentage to the whole area – and even predict from the sample where other sites might occur in the un-surveyed areas! Some pre-excavation surveys, especially in the USA, include finds from small trial holes – shovel test pits – to add more data to their results.

That's it – all the *pre-fieldwork assessment* and the first part of the *fieldwork strategy* has been completed, analysed and milked for all its worth. In some archaeological projects this marks the end point of the fieldwork, which then moves onto the publication stage. The results of surveys can be very productive and not every archaeology project involves actual digging. For many, however, excavation is the next stage. Time to find out just how many of those funny anomalies on the resistivity plot are pits, or whether that circular crop mark does surround a settlement. And time to refresh yourself about what ideas you had in your initial Research Design. Spades and trowels are cleaned, crews assembled and trenches laid out on the ground – time to break the ground in earnest and see what secrets it reveals. And keep in mind this celebrated archaeological advice:

It's not what you find, it's what you find out.

David Hurst-Thomas

3

The excavation

If we knew what was there, we wouldn't have to dig.

Richard Boisvert, NH State Archaeologist

There is one more thing to consider before you dig. In reality this would have been made explicit at the Research Design stage, but it still is useful to pause now and think about the ethics of the dig. First, excavation, even by a skilled archaeologist, is destruction. The trenches you are about to excavate can never be excavated again – that is a heavy responsibility to bear. Secondly, you need to have appropriate plans for the restoration of the site (in-filling of trenches) or the conservation of any remains left in-situ. Thirdly, you must record carefully and publish promptly – although, as noted, some fall at this final hurdle. Fourthly, you need to involve the local community and authorities in what you do. And lastly, you must have proper regard for the welfare and aspirations of those staff and volunteers who assist you – some of those will want to continue to work in archaeology.

▶ The dig

So you have ticked off all the ethical boxes, and feel suitably righteous. Time to dig! If your site is deeply buried you may need to use heavy machinery to remove the overburden. Most archaeologists employ a mechanical digger with a 'toothless' bucket, (i.e. one which has a smooth edge to the metal bucket that removes the soil) and carefully strip layers from a site until the first sign of archaeological deposits are observed. The skill in doing this lies in that last sentence. Remove too little and your workforce will be toiling for weeks digging through uninteresting deposits. Remove too much, and the tops of your archaeological features (and the finds that went with them) will be destroyed.

If you are lucky enough not to have to employ machinery, then it is time to lay out your trenches. Over the decades archaeologists have developed variations on a theme for this task. In the 19th century, excavators simply found a wall and then followed it. However, this technique destroyed the connection between the wall and the archaeological layers either side. Most now set out their trenches in squares or rectangles, sometimes in quadrants; often there are no trenches, just large open areas. Invariably a virtual grid is imposed on the whole site so trenches and finds can be located according to a co-ordinate system of eastings, northings and height or depth.

Now the art and skill of excavation is fundamentally straightforward. Imagine a box, filled with alternate layers of yellow sand and white chalk, each layer containing a different selection of artefacts. Your job is to remove (and number) each layer one by one, noting how thick or deep it is, and recover the finds noting their layer number and position. That's it – simple. In reality it gets a bit more complicated on-site, but the basic principle remains the same. The alternating layers of sand and chalk define what archaeologists call *stratigraphy*.

On many excavations every layer, such as a spread of gravel, or feature such as a wall, ditch, or post-hole, is given a unique context or unit number. Months later, when you are analysing a bag of finds, there should be an associated context number which will tell you from which layer the finds came. Excavated deposits consist of features, as well as layers. It can be useful to think about these features as either positive or negative. A positive feature, such as a wall or burial mound, is created on a surface, whereas a negative feature is one that is dug down through that surface. The construction of masonry walls involves both kinds of feature. First a trench is excavated to take the foundations for the wall – this is a negative feature and usually is wider than the wall itself. Then the wall is laid in stone courses – a positive feature. Once the wall is higher than the ground level the gaps between the wall and both sides of the foundation trench are back-filled with soil.

My friend and fellow archaeologist Peter Drewett made the obvious, but often overlooked, observation that people don't usually live on the tops of walls, or squat in ditches, but actually prefer horizontal surfaces. An excavator's job on a settlement site is to try and recover these horizons. Sometimes that is relatively easy. If you uncover a floor made up of tiles, or brick or a surface made from a layer of broken pot-sherds (I remember excavating one such outside a circular house in South Africa) then some finds on top of that surface may relate to the last period of use of that structure. But often houses have trampled earthen floors. In a notable example of surface-recovery Peter successfully demonstrated, by carefully recording the exact positions of all finds, that the artefact horizon that represented the living prehistoric surface, and activity areas within a particular house, was some 200mm below where it once was. Our industrious earthworms had sorted the finds to a lower level during the course of millennia.

Negative features, such as pits, post-holes, and ditches can be fun to excavate. In an ideal world, the filling of the feature is a completely different colour from the surrounding soil into which it was dug. Sometimes, when you machine-strip a site where the subsoil is an orange gravel, the filling of ditches shows up clearly as a dark, greyish linear band. Slowly peeling the grey soil back from the orange edges of the ditch can be both aesthetically tactile and therapeutic!

If the pit is big enough, or the ditch wide enough, you may be able to see different layers of filling and the process of excavation can be done stratigraphically, by removing and numbering the individual layers one by one. Often pits and ditches are small and the filling, to the naked eye, quite uniform. In these cases layers can be removed and numbered in arbitrary spits of 100mm depth. Some archaeologists use the terms *natural stratigraphy* and *unit-level stratigraphy* to distinguish these methods.

The square or more often round holes which once held wooden uprights or posts – hence post-holes – can sometimes be divided into at least four different contexts: the material of the post itself – usually a darker soil perhaps containing flecks of charcoal from the decayed post; the profile or shape of the post; the filling or packing of the post-hole around the post and finally the shape or cut of the post-hole. Often archaeologists record negative features by cutting a section across them. In the case of a ditch this simply means cutting through it at right angles so you are left with a vertical cross-section of the deposits filling it. With post-holes this technique does not work quite so well, especially when the actual post-impression is difficult to discern at the surface. The original post may have been placed off to one side of the post-hole and an arbitrary section may just clip it or miss it altogether. So it's best to excavate down in spits until the remains of the post can be observed in plan (i.e. horizontal) form.

▶ Detective work

Much of the detective work on an excavation involves discovering features. In the case of a masonry wall (a positive feature), that is easy enough. Sooner or later your pick-axe is going to strike something really solid – the facing stones or bricks of the wall. You might think that it is simply an isolated stone, but if you then find three or four in a line it may be something more structural. Soil-filled negative features, such as pits, ditches or robber-trenches (where wall foundations stones have been salvaged in the past), are a litlle more tricky to decipher.

It all depends on the contrast between the fill of the feature and the surrounding deposits into which it was once dug. If there is a colour separation, then identification is straightforward. But more often than not the contrasts are much more subtle, and sometimes can only be detected by a combination of observation and 'feel'. Some deposits – such as rubbish dumps or middens – can even smell distinctive. Some only appear after heavy rain showers, since different soils will dry out at different rates. A word of warning! Even excavation directors have their pet theories, their pre-conceived ideas. It is not unknown, when a rectangular or circular building is missing a couple of post-holes, for these to be detected by an all-seeing director while to everyone else on site they remain invisible! Remember that archaeological excavation is a slow process.

▲ Excavations under way at the Roman town of Silchester in southern England in 2013. The person standing to the right is drawing a feature using a square grid-frame placed over it as a guide.

> Dig, Dig! Cos the normal stuff's kinda slow, then
> they say we've found stuff! Archaeologists, you
> found stuff? What have you found, what have you
> found? Well, give us a toothbrush and ten years
> and we'll tell you. Give you a toothbrush and ten
> years and you'll tell me?!
>
> *Eddie Izzard*

▶ The finds

The 'finds' are crucial to any excavation. These are the materials you take away from the site – pottery sherds, animal bones, flint flakes, fragments of metalwork, small pieces of charcoal, carbonized cereal grains and so on. Some sites produce hardly any – a shoe-box full if you are lucky – others enough to fill a warehouse. Your recovery strategy for finds should have been made explicit in the Research Design.

Some artefacts you will just identify by layer or feature number; some might be recorded by a one-metre grid-square; some might be more accurately located in three dimensions by noting the eastings, northings and height or depth. On occasions you may want to recover very tiny items, say fish-bones, or small burnt seeds. This can be done by sieving all the spoil from particular features off-site and laboriously scrutinizing residues. Imagine panning for gold – but without the pay-off at the end! When it comes to personnel the skilled director will note that some people love this kind of forensic examination, while others will just get bored and miss vital finds. Choosing the right people for the right job affects the end results!

Taq and tpq

There are two terms you should familiarize yourself with, which date from the early decades of archaeology and which focus on the articulation of finds with features. These are known as *terminus ante quem* (literally 'limit before which') and *terminus post quem* ('limit after which') – *taq* and *tpq* for short. We will take an easy example to explain the difference. Imagine you uncover a complete tiled floor. Gradually removing the overlying deposits you reach the floor itself, and there, lying right on top of one of the tiles is a coin – and the mint date of the coin is 1485 CE. The coin constitutes a *taq* for the floor. That means that the floor must have been laid down prior to 1485 – or does it?

Remove a little section of the flooring and right underneath one of the tiles is another coin with a mint date of 1120 CE. The coin constitutes a *tpq* for the floor. That means the floor must have been laid down after 1120 – or does it? Now, if the coins had been dropped in those positions in the year of their minting then these propositions would hold true. But the 1120 coin might have stayed in circulation for a century and been dropped in 1220; and the 1485 coin might have been discarded in say 1585. So the actual date of the floor could be anytime, in theory, between 1220 and 1585. The golden rule for using finds to date features is to remember that the date (approximate or specific) of manufacture of the find is likely to be different from the date it found its way into the ground.

Human burials are excavated in meticulous fashion, the usual technique being to uncover carefully as much of the skeleton as possible, then record the body position and associated finds in detail, before lifting the bones and individually bagging the finds. It is a job for a skilled digger, not a novice. And it must always be done with care and sensitivity, especially if there is any real or claimed connection between the dead and the local community. There are particular ethical issues too that surround the excavation and retention of human remains.

But all archaeologists can make mistakes – so let me end this chapter by giving you a personal example. I directed an excavation once trying to date a large masonry city wall, by digging a trench up against it. Underneath the wall an intriguing small cavity appeared. At that point the curious boy took over from the experienced excavator and I pushed my shovel handle into the hole several times to see how far it went. Quite a way. Subsequently we found a human burial in a rock-cut chamber underneath the wall, and I spent a day in cramped conditions recording the skeleton of a juvenile who was accompanied in death by some exotic pottery grave-goods. I noted on my drawing a cluster of inexplicable small round depressions in the soil surrounding the bones. Weeks later these depressions continued to annoy me. The grave had definitely not been disturbed. Maybe an organic grave-good had been placed there and had decayed leaving no trace? Several months elapsed until I experienced a moment of exultant, if sheepish, revelation. The depressions had obviously been caused by my probing shovel handle. So if you ever see an excited excavation director poking a shovel handle down a hole – you now know what to say! Howard Carter, the discoverer of Tutankhamun, knew better:

> ... as my eyes grew accustomed to the light, details of the room within emerged slowly from the mist, strange animals, statues, and gold – everywhere the glint of gold. For the moment – an eternity it must have seemed to the others standing by – I was struck dumb with amazement, and when Lord Carnarvon, unable to stand the suspense any longer, inquired anxiously, 'Can you see anything?' it was all I could do to get out the words, 'Yes, wonderful things.'
>
> *Howard Carter*

4

Recording what you find

In a simple direct sense, archaeology is a science that must be lived, must be 'seasoned with humanity.' Dead archaeology is the driest dust that blows.

Mortimer Wheeler

Archaeology is very data rich. And you need a method to handle all this data. The information can come in many forms – thousands of layers or deposits, bags and crates of finds, hundreds of environmental samples, countless walls, floors, pits and post-holes. Remember that some seasonal excavations can go on for decades and you will begin to appreciate the challenge.

All this data needs to be analysed and summarized before it can be marshalled to support your interpretations. In the early decades of organized excavations, archaeologists used to keep day-books of what happened each day on the dig, often accompanied by preliminary ideas regarding interpretation and little hand-drawn sketches of key discoveries. Written in diary form these were quite charming records of an excavation, and frequently more revealing, full of anecdotes that wouldn't make it into systematized recording methods of the 21st century. Modern recording methods focus on objective description measurement and quantification.

▶ The recording system

One of the keys to a good recording system is to anticipate both what you might find on a dig, and to have different modes of recording intensity to match your recovery methods. It is obvious that if you are excavating an inhumation cemetery, then you need to make sure you have the very best methods for recording human bodies and associated grave-goods. Similarly, if you are excavating a Mesolithic (Middle Stone Age) camp, then your recording system might need to be geared towards the collection of small flints and bones, and environmental samples. Some excavators also define different levels of recording.

At the start of the dig, when you are removing extensive layers of soil manually, using pick and shovel, then finds might simply be collected by hand and all lumped together. Later on in the excavation discrete and thin layers in a ditch or a pit might be removed by hand, using a trowel, and the location of all finds individually plotted in three dimensions, with all of the soil then sieved to recover the smallest items.

Another critical issue relates to personnel. Your recording system, no matter how perfectly designed in the months leading up to the dig, will only be as good as the recorders themselves. Some people are better at doing the paperwork than others; some people are more accurate with drawing, others better photographers. Choose your record-makers carefully! Where paper recording systems a few decades ago were state of the art, most aspects of archaeological recording are now computerized, the data often being captured in the trench by a variety of digital hand-held devices.

▶ The context form

The building blocks of an excavation recording system are threefold – text, drawings and photographs. And a core component of the written record is usually a form designed to record the significant components of a single context (a layer or unit). Note that a context in most recording systems can also be a shape or profile, such as the cut of a ditch, pit or foundation trench; and it can also be an upstanding feature such as a wall. The context form summarizes the characteristics of the particular layer – its unique identifying number, where it is on site, its physical extent and depth. Usually it goes on to document the type of soil of which it is composed – sandy, silty or clayey – its colour, and then perhaps a general description of its appearance. This can be followed with notes on how it was excavated, and what sort of finds and samples were recovered.

Not all context forms are identical, but personally I like to see a space somewhere on the form for a note on how the deposit or layer was formed, and how the finds came to be in the deposit. Every single element recovered on an excavation, whether layer, pottery sherd or carbonized seed was deposited in the location you, the digger, found it by some sort of *formation process*. The soil might have been dumped there in a single episode, or it could have resulted from the slow accretion of wind-blown particles eroded from elsewhere. The pottery sherd could have been discarded there, or been carried out with manure from a nearby settlement to fertilize the soil. The carbonized seed might have blown there on the wind, or come from the nearby burning of stubble or processing of crops. These formation processes are interesting to speculate about, but the critical point is that you cannot move on to thinking about interpretation until you have gained a clear picture as to how things came to be where you found them in the first place.

A major element of any context form is a space for the provisional interpretation. Sometimes this is a straightforward description: 'north wall of Building B' or 'ditch running east–west to the south of Building B'. But sometimes the interpretation is less obvious, and sometimes people have different opinions. Interpretation itself is inextricably linked to discovery.

The recording system is meant to be 'objective', concentrating on 'the facts' much more than interpretation, which can come at a later and more leisurely stage, back in the office or study. However, human minds are not so compartmentalized, and it would be a strange director of a dig who did not think about interpretation almost from the point of discovery. They may keep their thoughts to themselves, or exclaim with some satisfaction that those two dark stains must be the missing post-holes for Building C, or that linear feature must be the long sought-after west side of Enclosure D. Nothing wrong with that you might think. But some directors are better at persuasive self-conviction than digging, and manage to convince everyone that those are indeed the missing post-holes or the long sought-after side of an enclosure. This belief might then dictate how those features are excavated and recorded. So a space on the form for something like 'the trench Supervisor didn't really think these were convincing post-holes' is a useful check.

Beware imaginative diggers!

This sort of premature interpretation fever can also grip the humblest of volunteers. In the archaeology of Roman

Britain many people have either read or heard of the notion that defensive ditches dug by the Roman army often had so-called 'ankle-breaker' slots in the bottom of them, whereas in reality these were the effect of repeated cleaning by teams of bored soldiers.

Sometimes, if you, as director, make the mistake of telling volunteers excavating a ditch that the feature might be a military one, some of the more enthusiastic of the band may take it upon themselves to discover the 'ankle-breaker' that will clinch your supposition. And, if you don't supervise carefully enough, one or two of the enthusiasts will actually manufacture and claim proof of an 'ankle-breaker' while your back is turned. You will be left looking at a slot in the bottom of the ditch and wondering whether it was dug some two thousand years ago, or is just two hours old! In this case look at the section, or side of the trench – there the ancient profile should be preserved intact, and act as a check on imaginative diggers!

A vital element of a context form I want to mention here is called the *Harris Matrix*. It takes its name from its inventor who developed it in 1974. It really is a simple way of recording, in diagrammatic form, which layers or contexts are later, or earlier, than others. You could use a Harris Matrix on the garden excavation example at the start of this book. It wouldn't be very complicated, just a series of boxes carrying context numbers joined by lines showing their stratigraphic (and therefore chronological) relationship to one another. Or you could use it to record a deeply stratified urban site running to thousands of contexts. The principle would be exactly the same. In the pre-digital age someone would have to draw these diagrams by hand, often on pieces of paper the size of bed sheets. Now a computer program will do the same in seconds – and, importantly, re-do it when you find you have missed out a context!

▶ Drawings

Drawings on an excavation come in two forms – plans and sections. Plans are depictions of contexts or whole surfaces in basically horizontal form. Some recording systems just require plans of individual contexts, others of areas that will show multiple contexts, and some use a mixture of both. The traditional excavation plan is usually at a scale of 1:20 (where 10mm on paper equals 200mm on the ground). Very often planners will use a one-metre square grid frame, strung out to make squares 200mm a side, and lay it on the floor of the trench. It is used as a framework to promote greater accuracy in drawing and to limit errors. Planning in this fashion takes time, and can be back-breaking work as the draughtsperson leans over the planning frame whilst gripping the drawing board. But in the right hands, the results can be superb, and better than any photograph. Sections are drawings of the vertical sides of a trench, or a cut through a ditch or some other substantial feature. Usually they are drawn at a scale of 1:10. They are particularly useful in recording the sequence of contexts, one above the other, to complement parts of the Harris Matrix. The digital age has transformed the equipment and on-site tablets and digital pens can now substitute for drawing board, graph paper and pencil.

▲ An archaeologist using an Electronic Distance Measuring Instrument to survey a site. Distance is measured by a signal emitted from the main instrument to the prism reflector, carried by the individual on the right.

▶ Photographs

The third major element of recording is photographic. Basically, on many excavations, everything of interest gets photographed. Some images are littered with information – such as an arrow pointing North, a scale, and a board providing the date and context number. All essential data when months later, or in some cases years, you want to identify that particular feature. However, cluttering the image in this way does detract from the substance and the aesthetics of what is being portrayed. So best to adopt a dual approach and do both types of photographic recording – one full of identifying data, the other without. Don't forget also to take plenty of images with people in them. Local people add colour, especially if you are digging somewhere quite exotic. Again, choose your planners and photographers carefully – most people can do both, but some are better than others.

▶ The finds record

The 'finds record' on an excavation is designed to cater for bulk finds and small finds. The former, large items such as tiles, pot sherds and animal bones, are collected and bagged by context number, and a bulk finds form can be provided for each context, describing in approximate terms the quantities and range of materials found. The small finds are usually artefacts such as coins, small pieces of metalwork and worked bone. They have an individual small finds form on which their exact location is noted, using the excavation grid system; space for a description and often a sketch of the object is also provided. Digital surveying equipment has made the capture of exact locational data much quicker and more accurate. When an excavation produces tens of thousands of small finds, plotting them out to form a distribution map, so you can see where all the coins or nails were found, can be a daunting exercise if undertaken manually. Thankfully, computer programs such as Geographical Information Systems can map out the data in seconds – leaving you, in theory, much more time to think about what it all means! Unfortunately, no computer programs exist at present to enhance your interpretative originality or subtlety.

Interpret the interpreter

Knowledge purports to be objective but is produced by humans, and therefore cannot be wholly free of subjective values. In archaeology this means how the prior experience and pre-conceived notions of the subjects (the excavation director, the diggers and volunteers) influence the way features are excavated and recorded, and the resultant interpretation.

Thoughts along these lines have been heavily influenced by postmodernism and the movement in archaeology labelled *post-processualism*. I have often wondered whether if two excavators dug exactly the same trench would they come up with identical results? I think there would be differences in data observed and collected, and much more so in terms of interpretation. So we need to know a little personal data, particularly about our excavation director. Where did they study? Who taught them? What have they published? Are they good at leading and involving everyone on site? And we need to know the conversations and discussions of excavation teams, the theories and counter-theories, as the dig progresses. The sort of information that doesn't find its way onto our 'objective' recording forms. These dialogues and observations are excellent material for a dig-diary or a blog. Often they prove more interesting to read than the formal excavation report! But only with them can we really judge the outcome of an archaeological undertaking.

I will tell you a little secret about archaeologists, dear Reader. They all pretend to be very high-minded. They claim that their sole aim in excavation is to uncover the mysteries of the past and add to the store of human knowledge.

Elizabeth Peters

Making sense of it all ...

We have to assume that the people [in the past] whose dwelling places, artefacts, lives even, we are dealing with were rational, integrated, sane and sensible human beings. Then we look around at our own contemporaries and wonder how this belief can possibly be sustained.

Laurence Flanagan, Ancient Ireland: Life Before the Celts

The digging season comes to an end. If it's a research excavation sponsored by a university or some such there is usually a sense of euphoria on the last day, which carries over into an end-of-dig party, a sort of rite of passage. A team of seasoned professionals, students and volunteers celebrate their success and camaraderie. Local communities are thanked for their help and hospitality. In the days ahead the team will disperse, and the director will be responsible for ensuring that all the finds, samples and records are carefully boxed and saved, and transported back to his or her permanent office. The excavation trenches are back-filled and the site restored to its pre-excavation appearance.

Now the really hard work, especially for the director, begins. Ultimately it should culminate in a series of publications in a variety of formats so what was found can be reported for posterity. But it may take years to get to that stage. First the various categories of finds have to be analysed. Each type of find – pottery, metalwork, glass, animal bones, charred seeds, charcoals, pollen samples – is sent to particular specialists skilled in studying that kind of material. Then, when the analyses are all returned, an overall interpretation of the site has to be formulated. These two stages are not so clearly separated, and often interpretation runs hand-in-hand with analysis. But it is through these two stages that the director struggles to make sense of it all, so we will look at them in turn.

▶ ^{14}C dating

One of the key things that people want to know about an archaeological site, whether a settlement, a layer within a settlement, or a burial, is how old it is. Before 1950 that could only be ascertained by inferring a date from the artefacts found associated with particular deposits. You could seek guidance on how old a pottery type or coin or bronze brooch was thought to be, and infer from that the date of your deposit. But there were problems with this approach, not least the fact that you were not so much interested in the minting date of the coin as in the date the coin was dropped into your deposit. All that changed with the development of absolute dating methods, the most common of which is radiocarbon dating or ^{14}C dating.

What is ^{14}C dating?

The principle behind ^{14}C dating is simple. All living organisms absorb ^{14}C while alive. They stop doing it the moment they die. The half-life of this radioactive isotope lasts thousands of years. So all you need to do is to measure how much ^{14}C remains in any biological sample and you can calculate how old it is. Archaeologists who, for instance, find charcoal, wood, or bone can usually derive ^{14}C dates from them.

Sounds straightforward. Not quite. Remember that for a piece of timber there is a difference between the date of the tree's death, and when that timber is carbonized in an archaeological deposit. And over the years there have been complications and refinements to ^{14}C dating, caused by the realization that there have been variations in ^{14}C levels over the millennia. Any ^{14}C date is also subject to a margin of error – a standard deviation.

There are other forms of absolute dating – some rely on the decay rates of radioactive isotopes, such as uranium, while others involve tree-ring dating (dendrochronology), dating of objects that have been subjected to heat in the past such as pot sherds or burnt flint tools (thermoluminescence or TL) and measuring the magnetic alignments in burnt clay walls of pottery kiln bases (archaeomagnetic dating). The beauty of such techniques is that they provide a date independent of other artefacts found in a deposit.

▶ Categories of finds

Some of the other categories of finds are more easily dealt with. The reports on pottery sherds, glass ware, metal objects and such like will eventually come back from specialists telling you what types and ages of pottery, glass ware or metalwork you have discovered, where the types were made and have been found before, and sometimes, if you are lucky, what they have been used for. Animal bone or charred seed reports should indicate the type of animals, their age, the identity of plants or crops, and will usually tell you something about what people were hunting, farming and eating. Analysis of pollen grains preserved in soil samples taken on site should give you some insight into what was growing in the local environment. If you are dealing with burials then analysis of cremated bone or skeletons from inhumations should provide clues as to ages and sex of the deceased, and perhaps some indication of the cause of death.

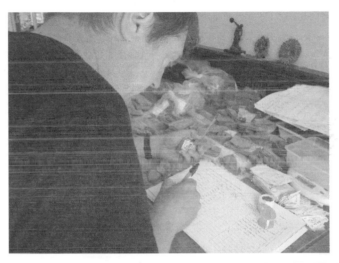

▲ Pottery sherds are frequently the most common find on archaeological sites. On most excavations every single fragment is recorded according to its size, weight, vessel type and fabric. From such accumulated tabulations inferences can be made about pottery manufacture, use, trade and exchange.

There is little on an archaeological site that cannot be analysed. A geologist may look at rock types found, and suggest which ones are local and which exotic (i.e. not-natural to the area), and therefore possibly imported. DNA analysis from human bones could decide if bodies in a cemetery were genetically related in life. Shell-middens, the result of accumulations of discarded shells from shellfish, will reveal the kind of shellfish consumed, the season of exploitation and the contribution to the diet. Land molluscs can suggest whether the local environment was a wooded or open one. Insect remains can be incredibly – and personally – revealing! Intimate relationships between pests and humans existed in Roman and medieval Carlisle as evidenced by the discovery of pubic lice; bed bugs were rife in Egypt of the Pharaohs. Insects are good indicators of climate change, too, since as sensitive little creatures they abandon or colonize habitats when conditions significantly alter. So the presence of ancient beetles has been used to suggest improving conditions which allowed humans to reoccupy northern Europe after the last ice age.

▶ Completing the puzzle

Imagine you are the director, say two years on from the end of the dig. You have files full of different specialist reports and hard drives full of analytical data. You have already worked out the main phasing of your site, and the kinds of major structures found. For instance, you may have identified the earliest dwellings as round-houses, which were superseded by two rectangular buildings, which eventually were abandoned – the land then being used for some kind of farming activity. The trick now is to merge the findings of your specialist reports with the basic structural narrative to provide a coherent chronological picture of human activities. Time to make sense of it all, or at least some sense.

Coming up with an overall interpretation of an archaeological excavation is like trying to complete a jig-saw puzzle, except that quite a few of the pieces are missing. That should not cause surprise given that what archaeologists dig up is only a small and biased percentage of what was once there in the past. On most sites organic remains (timber, leather, basketry) do not usually survive, and in most circumstances, when people moved away from a site they took their valued possessions with them. Excavators recover what was lost, or broken, discarded or deliberately buried, forgotten or that which survived later robbing – and they only usually recover a faction of that!

There is undoubtedly a difference between trying to interpret evidence from a prehistoric site (before written records) and a historic site (where some records pertaining to the site may exist). It might be thought that interpretation of a historic site would be easier, since documentary evidence might suggest what the name of the settlement was, when it was settled, what the rectangular buildings were used for and so on. The reality is more complicated. The author of the documents may have been writing a long time after the settlement was abandoned, and may never have visited the site. What looks like an authoritative comment or description could be quite flawed and misleading. Many an archaeologist has fallen into the trap of trying to reconcile the documentary evidence with the excavation evidence, and let the former dictate the overall interpretation. On balance it's best to consider the archaeological evidence in its own right, and then assess congruence or otherwise with any historical documentation. The relationship between archaeological and historical data is frequently a stormy one!

> After being an archaeology student for two years now, I can quite safely say I have learnt three things: First, you must NEVER like theory, or admit to even understanding it until you reach MA level at the very least. Secondly, all prehistoric archaeology students see themselves as the true archaeologists as everyone else cheats with [historical] text. Lastly, and most severe of all, archaeologists cannot abide historians.
>
> *Cath Poucher*

▶ Theoretical positions

Usually archaeologists start their interpretation from some overall theoretical position, although they may not all consciously conceptualize their theories at the outset. The approach that was popular in the first half of the 20th century can be described as *cultural diffusionism*. Basically it was assumed that each particular people or society in the past would be characterized by a unique combination of archaeological artefacts; these could be loosely termed different *cultures* or peoples. When pottery styles or building types changed it was assumed that this was effected either by the arrival of new people, or by some vague concept such as 'influence'. So, according to a 1930s analysis, rectangular buildings might have replaced circular ones because of the arrival of a new group of people, or the round-house dwellers decided, under 'influence' from adjacent people, that rectangular buildings were more suitable for their needs. There were multiple problems with these kinds of interpretation, not least the proof that each people or community can be represented by a unique combination of artefacts.

The 1960s saw a growing dissatisfaction with the old cultural diffusionist approach and the unsatisfying idea of 'influence'. A new generation of archaeologists, among whom the American Lewis Binford was a pioneer, sought to make archaeological investigation and interpretation much more scientific. They adopted the language of science, wanting archaeologists to formulate hypotheses and then go out in the field and test them. They encouraged the use of statistics and quantification in interpretation, and looked for definitive proofs that would ultimately lead to the formulation of laws that could explain human behaviour in the archaeological past. The American archaeological tradition has always been much closer to anthropology and Binford studied surviving peoples who still lived by hunting and gathering so he could make connections between people's behaviours and how the archaeological deposits were formed. This assumes, of course, that present-day surviving traditional communities, now often marginalized, resemble in some way those in the distant past. This movement came to be known as the New Archaeology. In the example quoted above, in the 1960s, round-houses and rectangular buildings might have been analysed for their respective structural efficiencies and ease of maintenance. People might have eventually preferred the latter because they were easier to build or use.

The 1980s saw the rise of a new theoretical movement – called rather opaquely *post-processualism* – which rejected the empirical approaches favoured by the New Archaeology. It was largely a British development. As part of more widespread concerns affecting society in general, post-processualism was fuelled by a loss of faith in scientific methodologies and their claims of impersonal, objective truths. Post-processualism also argued against the tendency to propose large, over-arching, narratives in archaeological interpretation. Rather it championed the role of the individual, and particularly the ability of the latter to change how societies or communities behaved. In terms of artefacts an emphasis was placed on the symbolic role of objects, and the way objects could influence human behaviours, rather than a concentration on their functions or decorative attributes. Again, returning to the above example, a post-processual interpretation might propose, in terms of round-houses, congruence between circular forms of architecture and a general equality of status among householders, while those living in rectangular architecture might be more disposed to accepting hierarchical differences.

The reality for the director writing the overall site interpretation is that elements of all three major theoretical positions probably influence the conclusions. Many of the specialists' reports will have utilized quantification and be couched in scientific terms. There may be some lingering suspicion that rectangular buildings did replace round-houses because of a growing 'influence' from a neighbouring power. And the director may wonder whether that the change from circular to rectangular architecture must have been preceded by shifts in local ideas of how people should live together and relate to one another. The director may also be conscious of his or her own biases, and the fact that some of his staff have alternative interpretations of aspects of the excavated site. Perhaps these alternative views should be publicised so readers can make up their own minds?

With so many options to consider, and so many perspectives to take into account, it is no wonder that archaeological interpretations are usually qualified with caveats, and examinations of competing possibilities. I remember an apocryphal tale of archaeological publication from my student days. At long last a director managed to get into print a substantial and eagerly awaited tome on a major excavation. After a couple of years the volume was reprinted, this time with the inclusion of a small *erratum* note. It simply said 'For possibly read probably and for probably read possibly'! Perhaps it's time to reflect more on how archaeologists have gone about the tricky reconciliation of archaeological data and archaeological interpretation. For instance, how do archaeologists fare when trying to identify and interpret the remote lives of hunters and gatherers?

6

The first people – hunters and gatherers

Hunter-gatherer societies also show that people can live in a co-operative way, without bosses or governments.

The Socialist Party of Great Britain

The following four chapters in this book explore four major types of society reconstructed by archaeologists: people who lived by hunting, gathering and fishing, and their spread across the habitable parts of the earth; the rise and dispersal of societies who adopted farming; the emergence of hierarchical chiefdoms and subsequently the appearance of states. Although it is tempting to read these chapters as some sort of progressive and evolutionary sequence, that temptation must be avoided. There must have been many instances when societies turned to 'simpler' forms of social and economic existence. The collapse of the western Roman Empire, or the putative environmental degradation and increased hostilities on Rapa Nui (Easter Island) are just two examples where circumstances dictated a reversion to 'simpler' lives. But we must be cautious when using that adjective 'simpler' when comparing societies. In the Western material world 'a simpler way of life' is often equated with a less material existence. Studies of surviving hunters and gatherers, however, have demonstrated that people can be materially minimalist but still enjoy very complex social lives.

▶ Examining the evidence

Archaeologists trying to reconstruct the livelihoods of ancient hunters and gatherers do not have much to work with. Generally the sorts of things they find are scatters of stone tools and some fragmentary animal bones and from these components entire lifeways need to be imaginatively reconstituted. Just occasionally the archaeological record is illuminated by an extraordinary discovery, such as a human burial or 'art', for instance cave paintings or engraved bones, produced by ancient hunters and gatherers. But usually the archaeological traces are meagre compared with those from more materially rich social groups. Faced with such evidence archaeologists turn to ethnographic accounts of extant hunters and gatherers to shed light on the chipped stones and broken bones in front of them. Comparing the ethnographic present with the remote past is not without its problems, however, not least that you run the risk of falsely reconstructing the past in the guise of the present.

▲ A Kenyah hunter from Borneo, where hunting wild animals, fishing, gathering nuts and berries and collecting honey provide key supplements for a diet that includes clearing patches of forest to grow dry rice.

If there was one moment in the 20th century when a seismic shift occurred in how we all view past and present hunters and gatherers it was 1966 at the University of Chicago. There some 75 archaeologists and anthropologists met to debate the current state of hunter and gatherer studies, eventually putting their thoughts in print in a ground-breaking volume entitled *Man The Hunter*. The book was edited by two Harvard scholars – Richard Lee and Irving DeVore – and their findings still reverberate today.

Man The Hunter reminded its readers that for 99 per cent of human existence we have been hunters and gatherers. It challenged two long-standing beliefs – one, that these people were very reliant on game hunting, and two, that their livelihoods were both arduous and precarious. Instead studies of surviving hunters and gatherers demonstrated that plant and marine resources were far more important than game animals. In addition, it was almost a truism that men hunted while women gathered, for example, nuts, wild plants and tubers. Lee and DeVore spent 15 months among the !Kung Bushmen of the Kalahari Desert (Botswana). They found that on average men and women 'work' about two to three days per week, but that it was the gathered resources that contributed most to the diet. A particularly important local food source was the drought-resistant mongongo nut. Its abundance and reliability ensured that Bushmen had no desire to imitate the more labour-intensive agricultural lifestyles of the farmers who surrounded them. When a Bushman was asked why he hadn't taken up agriculture, he famously replied:

'Why should we plant when there are so many mongongo nuts in the world?'

Richard Lee and Irving DeVore

▶ The early human species

With these thoughts in mind we can journey back in time about as far as the archaeological record will allow to reveal the faint traces of our earliest ancestors. An appropriate date for the beginning of human history is roughly six million years ago, the date of the last common ancestor of modern humans, *Homo sapiens*, and the chimpanzee. These early human, or hominin, species were ape-like creatures, partially walking on two legs, and probably living in East Africa before spreading to other parts of that continent.

Some of the sites producing the earliest archaeological evidence in East Africa are in present-day Ethiopia, Kenya and Tanzania. They usually consist of worked stone artefacts of lava, chert and quartz, sometimes associated with fossilized animal bones and occasional hominin bones. The stone tools appear to be for chopping up animal carcasses, with some of the animal bones displaying cut marks and abrasions from those tools. In Olduvai Gorge (Tanzania) the association of stone tools and scored animal bones has given rise to an on going debate about the significance of this relationship. Did early hominins purposively hunt animals and bring back parts of their quarry to a camp for processing and consumption? Or did they observe other carnivores killing and eating prey, with the leftovers being scavenged by hominins for scraps of meat and bone marrow? There is no definitive answer as yet, but the reality is that there was probably a whole spectrum of opportunistic and premeditated behaviours.

Our hominin ancestors eventually made it out of Africa shortly after two million years. Routes probably included a northwards migration up the East African Rift Valley and then onto the Nile and Jordan valleys. An additional sea route, crossed by simple raft, was available between North Africa and Europe. An intriguing question about their diaspora is whether they simply dispersed north from Africa as did large mammals, or whether there was something uniquely different about hominin behaviour. Even in that remote period, before the emergence of modern humans, were hominins motivated by curiosity, adventure and discovery?

The species we humans all belong to, *Homo sapiens*, evolved in Africa between 200,000 and 150,000 years ago. Since closely related animals such as chimpanzees make and use tools, the key markers of modern human thought and behaviours are taken to be predilections for complex technology, economic specialization, art, symbolism and, above all, language. We can anticipate that these signatures were present among the occupants of Blombos Cave in South Africa some 70,000 years ago. Here shell necklaces, bone points and a red ochre 'crayon' engraved with diagonal lines suggest an appreciation of aesthetics and ornamentation.

▶ Modern humans

Sometime after 150,000 years ago modern humans, like their hominin predecessors, made it out of Africa. They seem to have spread into south-east Asia much quicker than their more gradual colonization of Europe. An explanation may be the relative ease of travel and foraging along a very long coastal land-bridge between East Africa and the south-east Asian islands. Remarkably, modern humans were present in Australia by at least 40,000 years ago, and perhaps even 20,000 years before that. Rock shelters in Arnhem Land, Northern Australia, have produced contentious evidence for the earlier date. Not everyone agrees. Some archaeologists think that the stone 'tools' from these sites were really fractured by natural processes, while others argue that the tools have moved downwards in the stratigraphy, through natural processes over time, ending up in much older layers. What seems certain is that there was a fairly rapid movement of early human groups around the coasts of Australia. Several sites in Tasmania indicate that human groups had reached that island by 35,000 years ago.

Some 10,000 years before that a new type of stone tool technology, found in the Near East and Europe, almost certainly heralds the arrival of *Homo sapiens*. A recurring collection of artefact types – stone scrapers and blades, and antler and bone spearheads – suggests a much more sophisticated material culture and a more developed cultural world. Two routes were probably taken into Europe – one along the Danube into central Europe, while a southern dispersal followed the

Mediterranean coast into northern Spain. Both routes eventually brought the newcomers into contact with a much earlier hominin species – the Neanderthals – who had been in Europe for more than 200,000 years.

The rise of *Homo sapiens*

A controversy has raged in archaeology as to whether the appearance of *Homo sapiens* led to the extinction of the Neanderthals. It seems an obvious conclusion to draw, but there may have been other factors such as climatic changes that favoured the expansion of modern humans. Whatever the specific causes *Homo sapiens* eventually developed a richly symbolic culture in Europe. From about 30,000 years ago the archaeological record reveals ornate human burials, painted caves like those in the French valley of the Dordogne – depicting human forms, aurochs (wild cattle), horses and reindeer – bone carvings, figurines and even musical instruments. We know little about the social organization of communities from this still remote period. But what is clear is that these people had the time to develop elaborate ideas about life, death and the world of spirits beyond their conscious perception.

▶ Climate change

Planet Earth was, however, about to bring a gradual end to these lifestyles. The global climate began to cool from 30,000 years ago and ice sheets expanded from both North and South Poles. With so much water trapped in ice sheets, sea levels dropped, revealing and re-shaping landscapes. Britain was joined to the Continent, New Guinea to Australia and Siberia to Alaska. Forests in the high latitudes became scrub, while savannah in the lower latitudes became desert. Most of northern Europe was abandoned by human groups, save for some sheltered valleys in southern France and northern Spain where communities survived, evidenced by cave walls adorned with paintings. The ingenuity that characterizes, and perhaps explains the success of *Homo sapiens*, served them well. On the treeless Russian plain bands of hunters fed off mammoths, using their massive bones for fuel and as frameworks for skin-clad dwellings, as the discoveries at Mezhirich testify.

Global warming commenced around 15,000 years ago, melting the ice, flooding low-lying landscapes and re-establishing tree cover in the northern latitudes. Temperatures rose gradually but not continuously, with a particular return of cold conditions around 12,000 years ago. But the warmer climate returned and remains with us to the present day. Northern Europe was slowly re-colonized, perhaps in two distinct 'pulses' – by some hardy pioneers in the first instance, and then, generations later, by families and whole communities.

▶ Arrival in the Americas

One of the great debates in this final peopling of the world concerns the arrival of humans in North and South America. It used to be thought that a key site was at Dent in Colorado, dated to *c*.11,000 BCE. People living there manufactured large bifacial flint points (called Clovis Points from the type-site in New Mexico) with which they were presumed to have hunted mammoths. They were also supposed to have descended from ancestors who had trekked across the land-bridge from Siberia to Alaska and made their way south through an ice-free corridor. However, there have been a number of claims for earlier sites for human occupation in the Americas over the last fifty years, the most convincing of which is Monte Verde in southern Chile. Discoveries here of timber-framed dwellings, plant and animal remains and a variety of stone artefacts appear to be at least a thousand years older than the Clovis sites.

There is a huge interpretative problem, however, with trying to tell a believable story that links the Clovis Culture and Monte Verde. Since crossing by the Siberian-Alaskan land-bridge was only possible after 13,000 BCE this gives a remarkably short time (hundreds of years) for hunters and gatherers to have travelled all the way to what is now Chile. The logical inference is that the 'Clovis First' hypothesis is wrong and that modern humans had entered the Americas prior to their closure by expanding ice sheets, i.e. prior to 20,000 BCE. But the difficulty with that suggestion is that there are very few possible sites in North America which demonstrate occupation prior to Clovis. Studies from sister disciplines such as linguistics and genetics have failed to resolve this conundrum – so this problematic issue remains.

One popular image of hunters and gatherers in North America in the last 10,000 years is that of the dramatic bison hunts on the Great Plains. These certainly existed, as the 125,000 buffalo remains from elaborate bison jumps, such as the site called Head-Smashed-In, Alberta, indicate. Here bison were deliberately stampeded over a precipice so hunters would later carve up the carcasses. But the reality was that securing food was a much more varied business. At Barton Gulch in Montana there is not a single bison bone. Here the people focused on gathering plants and taking small game, such as rabbit, porcupine and deer. Bison were important, no doubt, but rather as a winter mainstay than an all-year-round staple.

▶ Voyages of discovery

The final episode of human expansion comprised voyages of discovery. From the Bismark Archipelago north-east of New Guinea humans intermittently sailed to settle in the islands of the South Pacific. The near islands, like the Solomon Islands, were reached as early as 30,000 years ago by people who left archaeological evidence for shark-fishing and shellfish gathering and introduced new species such as the bandicoot, sometimes referred to loosely as a pig-rat, and the Pacific almond. These introductions are interesting in that they provide evidence for an intentional addition to the local food resources. The more remote islands, such as Fiji, Tonga and then even further to New Zealand and Rapa Nui (Easter Island) were only settled starting from about 1500 BCE by people who were already horticulturalists.

The expansion of modern humans after the retreat of the last ice sheets, viewed from the distant perspective of the 21st century, seems like archaeological proof of the ability of our species to adapt to novel environments and experiment with new materials and ideas. It cannot have been a uniformly successful expansion. There must have been countless episodes of disasters, retreats and intermittent violence between groups competing for the same environmental niche. But gradually and cumulatively it was relentless. The variety of lifestyles, and the sizes of communities, must have differed enormously. The peculiar triangular houses of the fishermen who lived at Lepenski Vir, on the banks of the Danube in Serbia, demonstrate a specific adaptation, as do the groups who relied on salmon fishing on the west coast of Canada. At coastal sites in Scandinavia people relied on shellfish, seals and swans, but their differential treatment of the dead suggests different statuses in life, and their use of pottery marks them out as largely sedentary hunters and gatherers. In the Near East, at sites like Ohalo II in the Jordan valley, back as far as 18,000 BCE, a sedentary community exploited a full range of animals and fish, but also over 100 wild plants, including acorns, emmer wheat and barley, quantities of which were stored for winter consumption.

Bearing in mind the less-than-fulltime hours that the !Kung Bushmen put into their quest for food, we can only imagine how un-intensive life may have been for those living at Ohalo or Lepenski Vir, or on the coasts of Scandinavia or British Columbia. These were the well-off, members of original affluent societies, and people who seemed to have worked a lot less hours than we do to make ends meet. From *Man The Hunter* again:

> ... we are pleased to consider this happy condition [an affluent society] the unique achievement of industrial civilization [but] a better case can be made for hunters and gatherers, even many of the marginal ones spared to ethnography.

> *Marshall Sahlins*

7

The archaeology of the first farmers

Your corn is ripe today; mine will be so tomorrow. 'Tis profitable for us both, that I should labour with you today, and that you should aid me tomorrow.

David Hume

▶ The origins of agriculture

In 1970 a small book was published by the British Museum. It was entitled *The Neolithic Revolution*, and was written by Sonia Cole. It detailed the orthodox thinking of the time on the origins of farming in the Neolithic or New Stone Age. Simply put, hunters had started to turn to agriculture sometime before 8000 BCE in the Near East. The principal plants cultivated were cereals (wheat and barley), pulses, flax and fruit. Independently, farming had also appeared in the Far East (based on rice and millet) and in Central America (maize). Viewed from the perspective of the 20th century, the relatively sudden emergence of communities who lived on agricultural products derived from domesticated plants and animals appeared akin to a 'revolution'. People could now adopt a more 'settled' way of life, as opposed to a nomadic one, or one which necessitated seasonal movements of camp. Their food sources were now more assured; villages and towns could now support traders and craft-workers; new crafts such as potting, weaving, and polishing stone axes were developed; some communities even had the surplus labour to construct monumental tombs for some of their ancestors; farmers grew in numbers and spread out from centres of domestication. An example from the ethnography of New Guinea provides a charming example of the process of domesticating a pig:

> Young pigs are treated as pets. As soon as it is weaned a baby pig begins to accompany its mistress to the gardens each day. At first it is carried. When it gets a little older it is led by a

leash attached to its foreleg, but it quickly learns
to follow its mistress in dog-like fashion and the
leash is removed.

Roy Rappaport

The transition from foraging to farming meant that
human beings had emerged from the depths of the
forests to work sunlit fields full of ripening corn. Life
was good – the future beckoned! Or so it seemed.

That was 1970 and now is 2014. In a generation of
archaeological research much has changed regarding our
thinking on the origins of agriculture, a way of procuring
food that still works, albeit unevenly across the world,
pretty well today. Some elements of the story in 1970 are
still there but the mood music behind this fundamental
prehistoric transition has altered. The beginning of farming
provides an interesting case study in the development of
archaeological thought. That development, of course,
continues. In another thirty years or so this chapter would
need a lot of re-drafting, perhaps a complete re-write. In
what follows I want to touch on three aspects of the debate:
the archaeological methods and nature of the evidence
used in the study of early agriculture; the emerging picture
from several regions around the globe; and the crucial
question – just why did some people start to farm?

▶ Physical evidence

The nature of the evidence for early farming is varied
and fragmentary, and the methods needed for its
study call on a range of scientific methodologies. The

most direct source of archaeological information is the physical remains of the first farmers themselves, whether cultivators or pastoralists. In exceptional cases of preservation, such as very dry or very wet conditions, when a body is found in a bog, for example, then the actual contents of the deceased's last meal may still reside in the stomach. But 'finds' such as these are really exceptional. More common is the survival of human teeth on which the amount of wear and indications of disease can suggest a gradual change in diet, such as that derived from farming as opposed to hunting. Diet also alters the chemical makeup of our bones, and comparisons of nitrogen isotopes in human bones can be used to suggest a greater reliance on terrestrial as opposed to marine foods. Similarly levels of carbon isotopes can distinguish between cereals needing warm conditions and lots of sunshine (such as maize, millet and sorghum) and those that need less (wheat, barley and rice).

Fundamental types of evidence are the fragments of animal bones and plant remains discarded by early farmers. They can obviously indicate the relative proportions of domesticated animals, and the types of food plants being harvested. A big breakthrough in recent years, certainly not available in 1970, has been the development of techniques to retrieve microscopic remains of plants such as phytoliths (silica particles) and starch grains. This really is revolutionary for it has allowed archaeobotanists to look for plant domestication in the tropics, where staples were likely to have been seedless tuberous plants such as yams and palms. Other exciting techniques are still at an embryonic stage. Comparisons of ancient and modern DNA in plants and animals should be able to indicate whether a particular species of animal was domesticated (i.e. gradually tamed from its wild predecessor) in one or several different locations.

Some types of archaeological evidence are still drawn on for early farming, albeit more tentatively. The old agricultural signatures of a more settled way of life – more sophisticated architecture, potting, craft specialization and polished stone axes – are still read as strong indicators of an agricultural basis to daily life. In particular high-powered microscopy can detect use-wear traces on artefacts to suggest if they were utilized to harvest cereals, for example. Even more sophisticated, gas chromatography and mass spectrometry can reveal traces of liquids (such as milk) in the fabric of a pot. However, increasingly it is surmised that some hunters and foragers in the past would have, from time to time, used the same artefacts as neighbouring agricultural communities – such as pottery – for various purposes. So material culture is not necessarily the litmus test it appeared to be decades ago. Having said that, however, some archaeological evidence still holds good for early farming. The discovery of an array of field walls or field ditches around a settlement is usually a reliable indicator of some form of farming.

Ethnography and linguistics

Finally there are two types of evidence, each with its own problems. The first is that drawn from ethnographic studies which describe the lives of farmers and pastoralists (and hunters and gatherers) living in un-industrialized regions over the last two centuries. These descriptions of mostly egalitarian hunting bands and slightly more hierarchical 'tribal' farming societies are rich in detail, and it is tempting to apply social models derived from them to the past. However, for the millennia in which the transition to farming occurred, there is archaeological evidence for ways of life – particular combinations of hunting/gathering/cultivating/pastoralism – for which no modern ethnographic counterpart exists. Some elements of the ethnographic present thus can offer guidelines to the past; but they don't offer all possible guidelines!

The second form of evidence, a controversial one, is the correlation of linguistics with archaeological evidence. The theory goes like this. In Europe millennia ago there existed widespread families of languages, each family having a shared ancestry having spread from a particular location or homeland. The archaeological record for early farming reveals widespread archaeological complexes of closely linked artefact styles. Again these archaeological identifiers in similar sets of material culture seem to have spread from different centres of origin.

There appears to be a good deal of correlation between the map of language families and the map of early farmers who enjoyed shared material culture styles. The map of language families therefore indicates the dispersal of early farming groups. Definitely a neat theory but not everyone agrees with the basic premise.

▲ A group of women from the Kgatla people of southern Africa thresh corn. The rhythmical unity of their efforts doesn't hide the fact that agriculture could be back-breaking work.

▶ Regional evidence

The regional evidence for early farming is now much more complicated than envisaged in 1970. The first issue concerns the timescales for the transition to farming – essentially it is now seen much less as a revolution, much more of a slow evolution. We have already seen the case of Ohalo II in the Jordan valley where wild forms of emmer wheat and barley were harvested. Interestingly the large numbers of eagles, buzzards and vultures in the faunal remains suggest that people may have started to tame raptors for falconry, to assist their hunting, as far back as 18,000 BCE.

Around 13,000 BCE the world's climate warmed and foragers at Abu Hureyra in Syria were harvesting wild wheat and barley, encouraging their growth by the removal of weeds, and hunting by driving gazelles into stone enclosures. This community may have been formally one of hunters and gatherers yet their food strategies included animal domestication and forms of early horticulture. After a short return to much colder conditions there was a dramatic warming of the global climate shortly after 10,000 BCE. In the Near East novel combinations of hunting, gathering, herding and cultivation developed. But there was no correlation between levels of architectural complexity and the emergence of farming. The spectacular decorated standing stones from the temple at Göbekli Tepe in south-eastern Turkey provided a ritual focus for people who apparently lived entirely by hunting and foraging.

The evidence from China, while less clear-cut, is likely to demonstrate a mix of hunting and farming practices in a similar timescale over the last 20,000 years, with the harvesting of wild millet in the north and wild rice in the south. In both regions communities used ceramic containers to store both their corn for consumption and planting while, as in the Near East, the dog had been domesticated as an aid to hunting. In the Far East, after 10,000 BCE, at Kuk in New Guinea there is evidence for a shifting cultivation system based around yams, taro, sago and bananas.

In many parts of tropical lowland South and Central America the first evidence for what is termed *dooryard horticulture* – involving disturbing ground to encourage useful plant growth, and moving and tending plants – probably emerged after 10,000 BCE. Plants involved included avocado, arrowroot and palm. An incredibly wide variety of plants was subsequently harvested and tended throughout the Americas: roots and tubers in the tropical lowlands of Central and South America; squashes and weedy plants in the eastern woodlands of North America. One argument is that the expansion of lowland forests as the climate warmed made foraging more difficult, and favoured alternative forms of subsistence base. In tropical West Africa the first indication of something like dooryard horticulture was discovered at Shum Laka rock shelter in the Cameroons around 2000 BCE.

The jury is still out on whether reindeer hunters in northern Europe after 10,000 BCE may have been practising some kind of loose herding, and even tamed horses to assist with their hunting. In summary the evidence for the earliest horticultural and domesticating practices has been pushed back at least 10,000 years since the 1970s, and the geographical 'hot spots' for the emergence of farming seem ever more numerous.

That last point is a telling one. Can we still believe in just a few centres or 'hearths of domestication', from which early farmers spread out, colonizing new lands and displacing/marginalizing hunters and gatherers? Increasingly, new discoveries suggest 'No'. In the 1970s archaeology students were taught that one of the cradles of cultivation was the so-called *Fertile Crescent*, a curving stretch of uplands bordering the valleys of the Tigris and Euphrates.

This was a key locus for research since it was known that the wild forms of the 'primitive wheats' – einkorn, emmer and barley, plus sheep and goats – are still found there today. However, the distribution of modern wild cereals, and sheep and goats, extends much further to the west (southern Europe), north (Black Sea and Caspian Sea borders) and east (Afghanistan and Pakistan). Some of these areas were (and are) more difficult to conduct fieldwork in than others, and it could well be that the Fertile Crescent in reality was a small part of a much more extensive geographical region, perhaps providing the background for multiple, independent sites for the appearance of agriculture.

A similar case can be made for other regions of the world after 10,000 BCE. There is a dearth of information for tropical West Africa and more fieldwork is likely to provide more widespread evidence for farming and pastoralism. Evidence from the Ganges valley in north-east India suggests that local foragers had initiated rice cultivation, rather than immigrants moving westwards from China. In southern India local communities began to harvest indigenous millets and pulses, and domesticate zebu cattle. In short, the old theory of a few 'hearths of domestication' is likely to be overturned as more research in other parts of the globe demonstrates more and more separate instances of the slow transition from hunting and gathering to partial or complete adoption of horticulture and pastoralism.

Let's take a final look at theories of c.1970. A simplistic and popular notion was that the farming way of life had eventually spread across much of the earth through waves of colonizing agriculturalists who had migrated from the 'hearths of domestication', cultivating new lands and displacing or incorporating bands of hunters and gatherers. However, increasingly, radiocarbon chronologies have demonstrated, in Europe, Africa, the Americas and Asia, that farming appeared at irregular intervals and not in a smooth chronological progression from one direction to another. It appears much more likely that existing populations of foragers experimented with early forms of husbandry or adopted elements of farming from near-neighbours, rather than pioneer farmers displaced hunters.

Moreover the archaeological record for the transition to farming has become more kaleidoscopic. There are instances of foragers adopting some Neolithic (New Stone Age) trademarks, such as pottery, but maintaining their hunting and gathering lifestyles. Others tinkered with elements of horticulture or animal husbandry for millennia before pursuing more intensive agriculture. And it wasn't all one-way traffic. There are examples of foragers who became farmers and then reverted to foraging. An interesting observation on the gradual adoption, spread or independent take-up of elements of farming is that the change may not have occurred always because of 'economic' reasons. For instance, in the Mississippi region women married outside their own communities and may have taken harvesting and processing skills in maize with them to their partner's settlement.

▶ Why was there a transition to agriculture?

Lastly, that crucial question: why did communities, some after 20,000 BCE and many more after 10,000 BCE experiment with early forms of agriculture? Remember the Kalahari Bushmen who 'work' for only part of the week; farming there was a much more labour-intensive and time-hungry activity. It seems undoubtedly true that the background for the emergence of farming was one of climatic change: wetter conditions after 10,000 BCE allowed people to expand into the Sahara while temperatures rose elsewhere. Yet climate change was not the determining factor since human communities reacted to their changing environments in different ways. One theory is that individual households may have begun to tend certain plants and animals, not out of any desire to develop novel forms of subsistence, but in order to supplement their hunting and gathering livelihoods. Another theory is that the turn to horticulture was prompted by the desire for competition and social display. The pastoral Nuer of South Sudan prize their cattle above all else:

> ... this obsession [with cattle] ... is due not only to the great economic value of cattle but also to the fact that they are links in numerous social relationships. Nuer tend to define all social processes and relationships in terms of cattle. Their social idiom is a bovine idiom.

Evans-Pritchard

Cultivated plants could be fermented to produce alcoholic drinks for rituals and ceremonies. At La Emerenciana in Peru maize was initially a sacred plant, consumed as an intoxicant. Yet another notion is that some people began to think like farmers before they actually became farmers, first developing ideas about controlling 'nature' rather than being part of it. If I had to pick just one of these possible reasons for the slow adoption of agriculture I would suggest that it was because of hardship, when all other food supplies were diminishing, that people gradually began to tend plants and grow crops. After all, according to some, the first farmer, Cain (Book of Genesis), killed his brother, Abel, a nomadic shepherd, when God refused the former's offering of food grown from the land. Some scholars have suggested that this story is a parable for the conflicts between the nomadic and sedentary ways of life epitomized respectively by hunters and farmers.

In conclusion, the invention, adoption or transmission of food strategies based on tending domesticated plants and animals changed the face of the ancient world. In tandem with new subsistence practices population numbers rose, settlements grew in size and became more permanent, and networks of fields and cultivation terraces developed. New behaviours appeared in different regions – the construction of monumental tombs and meeting places, exchange and trade, the building of more permanent houses and storage facilities, more extensive quarrying for raw materials and the erection of edifices for rituals.

Those who were farming continued to live for millennia, sometimes in uneasy relationships, with neighbouring hunters and gatherers. Looked at from another angle, the case study of the origins of agriculture, whose practices continue to have a profound effect on the world today, provides a fascinating insight into how archaeological ideas can be modified over the timescale of a single generation.

8

Chiefs and chiefdoms ... the archaeology of inequality

'Shut up,' said Ralph absently. He lifted the conch. 'Seems to me we ought to have a chief to decide things.' 'A chief! A chief!' 'I ought to be chief,' said Jack with simple arrogance, 'because I'm chapter chorister and head boy. I can sing C sharp.'

William Golding, Lord of the Flies

The remorseless spread of agricultural and pastoral societies, and the progressive marginalization of hunters and gatherers, paved the way for increases in population and settlement size. More people crowding together in larger dwelling spaces created the circumstances for a few members of some communities to achieve higher status than others, for a minority to dominate the majority.

▶ Defining 'chiefdom'

In short, things socially, politically and ideologically became a lot more complex, and more unequal. Archaeologists and anthropologists have labelled some of these pre-state societies which displayed differences in wealth or status *chiefdoms*, and identified them in a variety of locations around the world – from Polynesia to North America. But some now think that the *chiefdom* label has been too widely applied, carries misleading overtones of social evolution (e.g. from tribe to chiefdom; from chiefdom to state), and, perhaps worst of all, is blinding us to other ways of interpreting past social forms. It's another intriguing tale of shifting archaeological interpretation.

A classic definition of a chiefdom can include a number of criteria: it controls a certain region, has a chief at its head, and its subjects, who can number a few thousand to tens of thousands, and are divided by status or rank. Status for the individual can be achieved by one's own effort; rank, a sort of official position in society, can sometimes be inherited. Chiefs themselves can gain supremacy by their own achievements or through being part of a particular descent group or lineage. Kinship and family connections are vital for an aspiring chief.

> A chiefdom is in a sense pyramidal or cone-shaped in structure ... A chiefdom differs radically from a tribe or band not only in economic and political organization but in the matter of social rank ... tribes are egalitarian, chiefdoms are profoundly inegalitarian. The most distinctive characteristic of chiefdoms as compared to tribes ... is ... the pervasive inequality of persons and groups in the society. It begins with the status of chief as he functions in the system of redistribution. Persons are then ranked above others according to their genealogical nearness to him.

> *Elman Service*

Chiefdoms could be simple or complex. Simple chiefdoms really only had one office – the Chief – and chiefs were only part-time office-holders, not spared the drudgery of food production. Complex chiefdoms had two or three layers of office holders and were able to support a class of warriors, build monuments, and control lesser chiefs in the near locality. Chiefs maintain their power by various means, one possibility being a claim to being close to the gods, another through the mechanism of collecting tribute and then giving it away to their subjects (often through large-scale events such as feasting), a third by controlling access to exotic prestige goods, and a fourth through control of a warrior caste. The archaeological evidence for a chiefdom might be a non-state society where there are particular forms of monumental architecture, where there are non-local prestige goods, and where grave-goods suggest that different grades of subjects existed.

▲ A son of the chief, from Samoa. The elaborate hair and head-dress emphasize the ritual importance attached to the head, and the necklace of sperm-whale teeth demonstrate power and esteem.

Chiefs did not necessarily disappear with modernity and the arrival of the modern nation state. In many countries chiefs have been recognized by national governments as a form of indigenous local authority. And they can still claim a special hotline to the supernatural. Very recently Chief Madamombe in Chivi (Zimbabwe) summoned Church leaders to his court to berate them for causing drought conditions in the area. The allegations were that Church members were holding their prayers on a hill which the Chief said was sacred because chiefs were buried there. The mountain was also used by villagers for their rain-making ceremonies. The case attracted widespread interest and a huge crowd gathered at the Chief's homestead for the hearing. Shortly before proceedings commenced there was a torrential and prolonged downpour. The case was postponed.

Circumscription theory

So why, and where, did chiefdoms appear in the first place? One prominent theory published in the 1970s, and dubbed the *circumscription theory*, was that chiefdoms and social complexity should emerge in agricultural areas where there were severe physical constraints on the amount of exploitable land. Think Nile valley, lush and green riverside lands annually flooded, and increasingly barren deserts beyond. In Polynesia chiefdoms seem to have emerged in difficult agricultural areas and then spread to lands with greater agricultural potential. A specific characteristic of chiefdoms is that they are not generally stable over the long term. They are prone to 'cycling' from simple to complex and back to simple. The reasons for such fluctuations include social competition, boundary maintenance and periodic warfare.

▶ Evidence for chiefdoms

Time to look at a few regions where chiefdoms are claimed to have been identified. In Barinas in western Venezuela an archaeological project documented the presence of chiefdoms. By the late first millennium CE it was possible to demonstrate population growth and defended settlements. At the site of Gaván an encircling earthwork protected a linear arrangement of major mounds and smaller house mounds. Lesser sites were examined which contained no mounded architecture at all.

At some sites it was possible to prove that variability in domestic architecture and mound size could be matched by differences in burial rites. Furthermore, some of this variation could be linked to the construction of canals, irrigation and drained fields that argued for a phase of agricultural intensification. In addition there was archaeological evidence for warfare and more extensive exchange systems.

Polynesia, with its scatter of circumscribed islands in the Pacific, has sometimes seemed as if it was a naturally made laboratory in which to observe the different trajectories of the growth of chiefdoms. All settlers in these islands were ultimately derived from members of *Ancestral Polynesian Society* (APS) who reached them by sailing from lands to the west.

The defining social organization of APS was that of a conical clan, with members defining themselves by descent and probably also through land-rights. Each community therefore was headed by a hereditary chief imbued with *mana* (supernatural power) from the ancestors and who was therefore *tapu* (sacred) as a result. This person formed a critical link between subjects, the gods, and the land and sea. Central to Polynesian food production was the tension between the requirements of the household, prone to underproduction, and the tribute demands of the chief. The coercive powers of the latter could provide the means for massive displays of military campaigning and ceremonial actions.

Although the first settlers on each Polynesian island carried with them the ideas nurtured in Ancestral Polynesian Society, and although each island was the location of population growth, the characteristics of each chiefdom were different. On Tonga the chiefs concentrated on storing agricultural produce and fostering long-distance exchange networks. Ultimately one lineage of related people became paramount expressing the importance of its central place by the monumental tomb mounds of Lapaha. On Hawaii, a large and fertile archipelago, a major theme of the several chiefdoms was one of conquest, territorial expansion, and then collapse. (Some even suggest that parts of pre-European Hawaii became a state – see the next chapter.) A unique characteristic of Hawaiian political forms was the peripatetic nature of the chief's residences, designed to spread the burden of demands for tribute more evenly.

On Rapa Nui (Easter Island), a relatively impoverished island, different chiefdoms and descent groups erected the famous groups of statues to commemorate their ancestors. Over-population may have been one of the factors that eventually led to the much debated environmental degradation and warfare, including the desecration and toppling of some of the statues.

The presence of chiefdoms seems to have been a truly global phenomenon. At the time of European contact most Philippine islands and coastal river valleys supported chiefdoms. These political institutions had not just arisen as a result of competition for prestige goods from places like China, but were the result of a long period of internal developments. Archaeologically chiefdoms have been largely demonstrated through the excavation of burials. The discovery of some extremely elaborate child burials at some sites has been taken as evidence of hereditary social ranking in lowland Philippine societies.

The United States is a particularly fertile ground for studying chiefdoms. The east, stretching from the lower Mississippi to the Great Lakes, during the first two centuries CE, was the location of the so-called 'interaction spheres' of the Hopewell culture. This was a huge region of different chiefdoms, or societies led by *Big Men*, who participated in an extraordinary exchange of prestige goods: marine shell and shark teeth from the south, native copper, silver and pipestone from the north, and obsidian from the west. These materials were fashioned into highly distinctive objects for ritual and decoration. Exchanged goods were utilized as grave-goods, and destroyed in ritual fires, patterns of activities that show consistency across a huge region. Impressive earthwork mounds of uncertain usages were also constructed, most notably in south-central Ohio. A veneer of cultural unity was created over the entire 'interaction' area where none had existed before.

▶ Challenging 'chiefdoms'

So chiefdoms seem fairly widespread geographically, and reasonably well-defined by anthropologists and identified by archaeologists, or so you would think. But not everyone involved in studying social complexity in the past is happy. Sometimes academic terms fall out of favour. The *Oxford Handbook of Archaeology*, all 1100 pages of its world-wide coverage, doesn't apparently mention chiefdoms, at least if the index is anything to go by! Partly this taboo on chiefdoms is a reaction against the social evolutionists of some fifty years ago who saw a progressive link from hunting bands to farming tribes to redistributing chiefs and finally to states and exploiting empires.

However, there are recorded instances of hunters ruled by chiefs, tribes that were the creation of colonial powers, the recycling of large to small chiefdoms and empires that reverted to competing chiefdoms. Partly there was also a circularity to some archaeological research projects that looked for the evidence of chiefdoms and, when finding differences in burial treatment, varying house types and sizes and the presence of exotic goods, used these to propose the presence of chiefdoms. Has the idea of chiefdoms become just a little too fixed in archaeological interpretation? Has it put the blinkers on our imaginations? Some archaeologists think so.

Africa, south of the Sahara, is a good place to start the deconstruction. There it is argued that chiefdoms simply didn't exist in the way they did in Polynesia or eastern USA. Instead power could be exercised through horizontal differentiation of people and by collective decision-making. Influence was distributed through a variety of horizontal social associations, such as cult groups, age-sets and secret societies, that cross-cut and restricted vertical divisions based on rank, descent or status. This is a non-hierarchical model for communities which sometimes resisted the consolidation of authority by ambitious individuals. Two archaeological cases will suffice as examples.

Non-hierarchical societies: the evidence

The Igbo of south-eastern Nigeria are grouped into over 200 separate village groups, each accommodating thousands of people, and each with its own internal organization. The inhabitants of village groups are divided into different lineages and trace descent in the male line. However, there are numerous age sets and secret societies which criss-cross lineage divisions. In theory, village decisions are made democratically through meetings of all adult males. There are prestigious positions and titles within the villages but these are open to all. The most remarkable testimony to ancient Igbo society is represented by the fabulous late first millennium burial and ritual bronze objects from the town of Igbo Ukwu. An individual was buried in a large pit seated on a stool, and accompanied by elephant tusks, a copper crown, pectoral, anklets and staff, cast bronze vessels and over 100,000 imported glass and carnelian beads. If this burial had been discovered anywhere else in the world it would have been taken as evidence of a chiefdom. But the excavator, mindful of Igbo ethnography, interpreted the deceased as a high status title holder in a non-hierarchically organized society.

The second example is an urban site – Jenne-jeno in the upper inland Niger delta – which flourished in the late first millennium CE. The town's inhabitants lived in round houses made of tauf, or puddled mud, and the settlement reached its greatest extent, some 33 hectares, by 850 CE. But the site does not fit the standard outline that characterizes complex chiefdoms. It has some of the familiar attributes, such as population growth and nucleation, but not others such as subsistence intensification, highly visible ranking or stratification, or imposing public monuments. This settlement, devoid of the archaeological markers for an elite sub-set of the population, looks like the product of a democratic society, not one ruled by chiefs.

There are other examples where the standard chiefdom explanation, controlling a locally bounded territory, doesn't appear to be a good fit, or has been challenged. Stonehenge in southern Britain, that long-lived monument which climaxed architecturally around 2500 BCE with the construction of the towering stone trilithons, arranged in a rough horseshoe-shape, seems to have been the burial place of some elite ancestors. The authority required to marshal the human labour to construct the monument looks like it could have been exercised by a chief.

However, the number of stone circles throughout the British Isles seems to imply a sort of pan-island connectedness, with Stonehenge cast as a monument of unification, the 'navel of the world'. The geographical and ritual reach of Stonehenge, and the supposed longevity of its attraction for distant communities, suggests some organizing principles that transcend the hierarchy of local chiefs.

Conflicting interpretations of pre-Roman Iron Age hillforts in southern Britain provide another example. Some interpret these as elite residences from which chiefs exercised authority over the farmlands that surrounded them, and regulated the flow of imported prestige goods. Others have noted that the architecture and material culture of some hillforts was little different from that in use outside the forts, while archaeological excavations and surveys suggest some hillforts were largely devoid of permanently resident inhabitants and structures.

A key zone for the study of chiefdoms has been the Midwest and south-eastern United States, home to the Mississippian period of mound centres and villages. Here chiefdoms, whose agricultural base rested on maize cultivation, dispensed authority from central settlements characterized by mounded earthworks and ancestral burials. Most mounds were small but some, such as the Monks Mound at Cahokia (St. Louis, Missouri), were truly monumental. The flat-topped mounds supported wooden buildings, including the houses of chiefs, community buildings for the elders, and charnel houses for the bones of ancestors. Objects made from precious materials, such as marine shell and copper, were buried with the dead. Patchy distribution of pockets of the most productive land supported individual chiefdoms. That is the orthodox view.

A challenge to the orthodoxy comes from a book by Tim Pauketat, provocatively entitled *Chiefdoms and other Archaeological Delusions*. In essence he bemoans the straightjacket the chiefdom model imposes on much of the archaeology of the eastern USA. In particular he makes the point that Cahokia was just too big, too early and too far north to fit into the context of standard Mississippian chiefdoms. Instead he argues that Cahokia looks more like a city, probably with a standing army, laid out according to some cosmic scheme, and enforcing a *Pax Cahokiana* (a play on the term *Pax Romana* – the 'peace' that the Romans established in their empire) throughout the region. Cahokia may even have been the capital city of a state or even an empire. The author seeks to remove those blinkers from archaeological interpretations with some fundamentally challenging questions about pre-white settler North America:

> No cities in North America? Why not? If a city is a relatively dense concentration of people disposed in such a way as to reveal central organising principles other than kinship, then Cahokia was a city, as least for about a hundred years (1050–1150 CE).
>
> *Tim Pauketat*

The questioning of the status of Cahokia is productively provocative, doubly so. By claiming that Cahokia could be a city the foundations of archaeological reconstructions of chiefdoms in the Mississippi are shaken. And by suggesting that Cahokia might have been part of a state, the self-imposed constraints of our narrow archaeological interpretations are shown for what they are – sometimes enlightening for sure, but sometimes all too restrictive.

9

The archaeology of states

They [the Romans] are the only people on earth to whose covetousness both riches and poverty are equally tempting. To robbery, butchery and raping, they give the lying name of 'government'; they create a desolation and call it peace ...

Tacitus

Undoubtedly the most complex of that quartet of socio-political categories – band, tribe, chiefdom, state – is the last. Before we look at some archaeological examples we must be clear, or at least as clear as possible, about the definition of states. Archaeologists in some parts of the world spend a lot of time and effort trying to assess whether this or that society in the past attained statehood.

▶ Defining 'states'

Defining whether a society in the past had achieved statehood is not an easy matter. No agreement has ever been reached on what constitutes a universally accepted general definition. Like the notion of a chiefdom, too rigid a definition is likely to act as a hindrance rather than a help. Perhaps the simplest idea of a state is a political entity that has fairly well recognized territorial limits usually (but not necessarily) over a wide geographical area, an organizational centre or capital (which can be peripatetic) from which a ruler or ruling group exercises political authority and maintains its rule over several generations.

I am not considering here a rather special kind of ancient state – the city-state. The latter consisted of an independent or autonomous entity whose territory comprised a city and possibly its surrounding territory. Rome developed into a city-state, but soon expanded to become the capital of a geographically extensive state and eventually an empire. Athens and Carthage in their early stages were two other famous examples of city-states.

There are some other often-cited ingredients in the make-up of a state. One concerns the use of coercive power – military force. In states this is invariably monopolized by the rulers who can use physical means to launch attacks on other groups beyond the state's boundaries, and thus form empires. Or they can use their soldiers or warriors to police unruly inhabitants within their own state, suppressing social or political disturbances with punitive strikes. Another key element of statehood is usually the formation of some sort of bureaucracy, or civil service. Importantly, and as a distinction from chiefdoms, the members of a state bureaucracy, who form an elite level within society, should have risen to their positions or been selected on

▲ The Arch of Titus just to the south-east of the forum at Rome. On its walls were carved scenes from the Roman sack of Jerusalem under the Emperor Titus in 70 CE.

merit, rather than have been allotted them because of some prestigious family connection.

A critical element of statehood is that the state needs to gain revenue from its inhabitants in order to pay for the costs of standing armies, wars of expansion, expensive public buildings and bureaucracies. This is one of the many transformations between chiefdoms and states. Chiefs extract revenue in the form of tribute and give a good deal of it back to the common people by way of redistribution in feasts and rights to land. Rulers of states change this tribute into a form of regular taxation. Taxation, of course, is one of the least desirable legacies of the emergence of states. Most of us begrudgingly pay them, and most of us have an opinion on them. Sardonic quotations about taxation are legion. One of my favourites is that from Jean-Baptiste Colbert, a French politician under Louis XIV: 'The art of taxation consists in so plucking the goose as to obtain the largest amount of feathers with the least amount of hissing.'

Rulers of states find that because of the costs of governance less of the revenues taken in tax revert back to the people. Instead the rising costs of states usually mean that the rulers encourage an intensification of agricultural outputs and more efficient exploitation of the state's resources. Alongside this is the necessary development of uniform weights and measures, and a system of recording and accounting. This all sounds as if a material requirement of early states was use of a standardized coinage and written records – but, as we shall see – neither monetization nor textual documents were a prerequisite for state formation.

One last point. States sometimes give birth to other states in a particular region. Purely to defend themselves against an expansionist state other large communities may be forced to adopt the forms of statehood. The Holy Grail for some archaeologists is to identify in which areas of the world, and when, the first or primary states emerged. Until not so long ago the usual confirmed suspects were Egypt, Peru, Mesoamerica, Mesopotamia, the Indus Valley and northern China. Now there are other candidates. Let's look at the archaeological evidence.

▶ China

Excavations at Erlitou in Henan province south of the Yellow River have taken place since 1959 and have unearthed a large city, measuring approximately 2.4 km by 1.9 km; seemingly the capital of a primary state. The city appears to have flourished from 1900 to 1500 BCE and given its name to a particular set of widespread material items known as the Erlitou culture. During the peak of its settlement the ancient city of Erlitou was partitioned into several sections with specialized functions. In the centre of the site was a palatial zone. The biggest palace in that zone comprised a single building, fronted by a large courtyard, erected on a rammed-earth terrace which was enclosed by walls. In the southern part of the city an area was dedicated to bronze working, archaeologically suggested by thick deposits of slag, remains of crucibles, clay moulds and castings. The clay moulds were used for casting tools, weapons and particular types of bronze ritual vessels, which were elaborately decorated. In the northern parts of the city bone workshops and potteries were located. The potteries seem to have produced distinctive three-legged white vessels, similar to some bronze vessels. Both bronze and pottery containers were probably used in drinking rituals and ceremonies facilitating forms of ancestor worship.

Chinese archaeologists have therefore documented key characteristics from Erlitou which they claim demonstrates statehood. These are a large urban population probably in excess of some 20,000 people; the establishment of a central complex of palaces; the development of various craft specializations; the evidence for different ranks and statuses in society evidenced by differences in grave-goods buried with the deceased; and the presumed state control of production of the elaborate ritual bronze vessels, which clearly formed the material component of a shared Erlitou ideology. The rulers of Erlitou also established dependent cities in distant regions so that a clear four-tiered settlement hierarchy emerged, another key characteristic utilized by archaeologists to define statehood.

▶ Peru

Another primary state has been suggested by recent archaeological work in the Virú valley, in coastal northern Peru. Here it is argued there was a valley-wide political unity, evidenced by the establishment of a four-tiered settlement hierarchy, including an urban centre of exceptional dimensions (the Gallinazo Group of mounds), mid-sized defensive settlements, villages and small hamlets – all associated with a comprehensive irrigation system. One of these mid-sized settlements has now been partially excavated – Huaca Santa Clara. Imposing storage facilities were located on its hillsides, as well as moderate-sized civic buildings. Radiocarbon dates from the site indicate that it flourished for several centuries between the 2nd century BCE and the 8th century CE. Huaca Santa Clara functioned as an important node in Virú's valley-wide administrative network of mid-sized settlements. Four of these formed a unified system of fortification at the neck of the valley, the only entry point from the Andean highlands and the source of water-intakes for irrigation canals.

The Gallinazo Group of mounds spreads over an exceptional 600 hectares of flatlands at the mouth of the Virú. Population estimates are difficult, especially as the domestic architecture on some of the mounds comprised thousands of contiguous small rooms crammed together in an agglutinative fashion. But the figure probably lies between 14,000 and 28,000 people. The archaeological evidence for an increase in population, for a growth in production capacity brought about by extensive irrigation and for a unified political command in the Virú valley evidenced by similarities in material culture, suggests that the valley was the location of a primary state, which probably emerged sometime in the 2nd century BCE.

▶ Africa

A candidate for a primary state in Africa might be the ancient kingdom of Ghana, south of the Sahara. It was located in what is now south-eastern Mauritania, northern Senegal and western Mali. Complex societies had existed in the region from about 1500 BCE, and around Ghana's core region since about 300 CE, indicating that the emergence of putative states in this part of Africa pre-dated Islamic contacts. A stimulus towards statehood was probably provided by the location of ancient Ghana at a cross-road of trade. Their cities and markets stood at the southern end of important caravan routes across the Sahara, established since at least Roman times, while they also stood at the northern end of routes that came from gold, ivory and salt bearing regions to the south.

There is evidence that the kings of ancient Ghana probably kept traders, especially foreign traders, under close scrutiny, sometimes confining them to their own separate towns. The tax revenues on which the kings grew fantastically wealthy derived from trade. Each trader had to pay a tax on any goods brought into, or taken out of, Ghana. In addition, it was declared that all gold found within the kingdom was the property of the king himself and therefore the king could control the amount of gold in circulation, preserving it for himself and his elite circle, and keeping the price high for foreign traders. It must have been hard to escape the glitter of gold at the royal court:

> The King adorns himself like a woman wearing necklaces round his neck and bracelets on his

forearms and he puts on a high cap decorated with gold and wrapped in a turban of fine cotton. He holds an audience in a domed pavilion...

At the door of the pavilion are dogs of excellent pedigree. Round their necks they wear collars of gold and silver, studded with a number of balls of the same metals.

Al-Bakri (10th-century geographer)

French archaeologists have been at the forefront of trying to locate the capital of ancient Ghana. A possible candidate – not accepted by everyone – is the early medieval town of Koumbi Saleh in south-east Mauritania. There, houses were constructed from a local stone (schist). From the quantity of debris it is likely that some of the buildings had more than one storey. The rooms were quite narrow, probably due to the absence of large trees to provide long rafters to support the ceilings. The houses were densely packed together and separated by narrow streets. In contrast a wide avenue, up to 12 metres in width, ran in an east–west direction across the town. At the western end lay an open site that was probably used as a marketplace. After the arrival of Islam the main mosque was centrally placed on the avenue. There were two large cemeteries outside the town suggesting that the site was occupied over an extended period. Radiocarbon dating of charcoal fragments from a house near the mosque has given dates that range between the late 9th and the 14th centuries CE, towards the end of ancient Ghana's empire. The French archaeologist

Raymond Mauny estimated that the town would have accommodated between 15,000 and 20,000 inhabitants although this is an enormous population for a town with a very limited supply of water in the Sahara.

Another obvious state in West Africa is that of the Asante; at the height of its powers it controlled an empire that stretched from Ghana to Benin and the Ivory Coast. Two resources underpinned the Asante state – the intensification of a rural economy based on subsistence agriculture and the exploitation of substantial deposits of alluvial gold. The kingdom was unified in the early 18th century CE and a Golden Stool became the symbol of political unity and regal authority. The capital was at Kumase, which had a population of some 20,000 to 25,000 people. Most of its citizens became gradually divorced from their agricultural origin and instead were involved in the transactions of government business, in the time-consuming performance of elaborate state ceremonies, and in the production of luxury artefacts for the elite. At the heart of Asante ideology lay a predisposition, for those who could, to accumulate wealth – in the form of gold, people, land and goods.

The British, who fought four wars against the Asante, and who destroyed part of the royal palace at Kumase in 1874, had long been impressed by not only the gold but the agricultural wealth of the kingdom. In 1848, at Kumase, the British Governor of the Gold Coast was presented with:

> 2 bullocks, 4 sheep, 4 turkeys, 6 ducks,
> 20 guinea fowls, 6 pigs, 20 fowls, 20 pigeons,
> 400 yams, 303 bunches of plantain, 4 dishes of

native rice, 5 dishes of ground nuts, 6 calabashes of honey, oranges, eggs, palm nuts, sundry vegetables; 40 logs of wood, 10 baskets of corn ... brought to me by 550 men, every one of whom had some share in the work of conveyance.

▶ Hawaii

The final example of a primary state is one that is not located in any of the classic greenhouses of political complexity like the Nile or Indus valleys, or the Mediterranean basin. Instead it comprises eight smallish islands forming an archipelago some 4,000 km south west of Los Angeles and some 6,000 km south-east of Tokyo. They were not even settled until sometime in the first millennium CE. Today we know them as Hawaii. So, how is it that Ancient Hawaii, which exhibits no urban development, no towns, and indeed few nucleated settlements that could be described as villages, merits the label of a 'primary state'?

Part of the answer to that question lies in efforts by archaeologists to understand the development of agriculture on Hawaii since the landfall of the first human beings. In the early period the dominant agricultural practices are assumed to be based on shifting cultivation. The first archaeological evidence for irrigated agriculture dates from c.1350 CE. The cultivation of irrigated taro was preferred over sweet potato and other rain-fed crops. Irrigable land on the main island of Hawaii was rare, however, and by the end of the late 17th century CE all possible irrigable land was under cultivation. In the century preceding European contact (c. 1680–1790) agriculture was intensified further using fields bounded by stone banks and hillside terracing to support rain-fed agriculture. Evidence from archaeology and ethnography suggests that such changes brought harder times for both men and women, rapid population growth, and diminishing productivity. These critical transformations provided the catalyst for unprecedented application of force in expansionary wars by some of Hawaii's chiefs, leading to the emergence of a state borne out of an agricultural crisis and over-population.

A particular cultural choice by rulers in Hawaii was to eschew the storage of large quantities of taro. The royal court was therefore a very mobile one. The king's advisors constituted a group of up to a thousand officials, priests, warriors, messengers and servants, as well as craft specialists. They all sailed in large fleets of ocean-going canoes and required no more than a few days to move from one island or region to another. Exhaustion of food supplies may have prompted some moves, but others were no doubt politically motivated to visit a subordinate chief who might have been fomenting rebellion. Armies could be recruited by the king's command and sometimes numbered as many as 15,000 men sailing in over a thousand double-hulled and outrigger canoes.

Other facets of the embryonic Hawaiian state include an accounting system that stemmed from the great annual ceremony of Makahiki, a four-month long celebration of rituals, processions, feasting and offerings asking Lono, the god of agriculture, to bestow plenty in the coming year. Tax collectors kept a very close tally of the amount of clothing, pigs, feathers and agricultural produce that each land-holding unit provided, along with a rough census of men from each community available for public works and military service. There was also a well-developed bureaucracy that allowed the king to delegate political power through at least five layers of chiefs. This was supplemented by a formal messenger service that doubled as a spy agency.

An early 20th-century recorder of Hawaiian folklore, Kamakau, cites the connection between food poverty, war and state formation for a chief called Kanaloa around 1640 CE:

> Kanaloa-kua'ana's ... priests, counsellors and people have clear urine because they drink copiously of water. That is because you are a poor chief. The urine of chiefs, priests and counsellors of a wealthy chief is yellow through drinking 'awa and eating rich foods. Their lights will never go out at night. The chief [Kanaloa] said 'what must I do'. 'Make war on 'Umi-o-ka-lani and take the whole kingdom to yourself'.

Two things emerge from this brief study of primary states. The first is the comparison with how archaeologists have redefined the emergence of agriculture, as outlined earlier in this book – moving from a few 'hot spots' to a more geographically widespread view on the appearance of farming. There is a sense that in a generation's time we might see the same in respect of the primary state. I suspect that many more will be found, particularly in Africa. The second concerns the fixing of inequality that states brought. As territories increased in size and as populations grew social classes became more formalized – slave, commoner, priest, craft-worker, land-owner, administrator, warrior, aristocracy – based less on kin and more on merit. As a result the opportunities for cross-cutting groups such as age-sets or family lineages to counteract the vertical commands of authority became less.

Most of us live in states now, and many of them are already quite long-lived. Most states, too, have varying degrees of literacy and a written record of their development and history. You would think, in terms of a study of the past, that the arrival of historians would herald the departure of archaeologists. The latter are surely not needed, now there is the written testimony of an eye-witness account, or a surviving chronicle of a particular period. But the archaeologist brings a particular material emphasis to interpreting the quite recent past. History and historians only provide a partial account of the past. Now let's take a closer archaeological look at the much more recent past.

10

Historical and contemporary archaeology

After all, the argument goes, why bother with archaeology if you can ask the people themselves, read historical documents, investigate census records? Don't we know enough about modern-day occurrences to make archaeological investigations a waste of time?

K Kris Hurst (from a book review).

▶ Historical archaeology

Historical archaeology usually describes the archaeology of the period from 1500 CE up to and including the present. It is a relatively new branch of the discipline, only really emerging since the 1950s. It is commonly associated with those countries where written documentation on the past survives; in which case archaeological research into a particular area or site attempts to combine, along with other strands of evidence, surviving material culture and documentary evidence. Sometimes these lines of evidence complement each other well, sometimes they are antagonistic. But it would be wrong to identify historical archaeology only with literate societies. In Africa, for instance, many historical traditions are recorded in prose, dance and song, orally transmitted between generations and the archaeological task is to correlate oral and material culture records. Many archaeologists tend to treat historical records as just another form of material culture, therefore giving written records no greater weight than excavated material.

It is a truism, however, that most surviving written records provide only a partial and biased account of events or locations in the past. The bias usually stems not from any attempt to mislead but from the fact that what things were written down depended on the selectivity of those requesting a written record and of the scribe or author themselves. Many documents are testament to the power of the middle or upper echelons of society, whereas archaeological finds can be much more undiscriminating.

If you want to listen to the voice of the repressed and dispossessed, you are more likely to discover it in the mundane objects and buildings they left behind.

A good example of the different focus provided by historical archaeology comes from the American South. Minimal documentary records indicate that one Sylvia Freeman was born into enslavement in Virginia in 1855. She may have been sold to an owner from Louisiana, since there is a record of a marriage. In 1900 census records indicate that she is a widowed cook, and her plantation owner records her salary, monthly purchases and cash advances. There is no written record of her death, or any surviving will. However, the excavation of her house, which was raised on brick piers, allowed the recovery of a great number of small items that had either slipped through the floorboards or been swept as trash underneath. These artefacts provided a much more richly textured, personal and continuous insight into Sylvia's life than the meagre official surviving records allowed.

Urban sites are a key focus of research for historical archaeology. The documentary records are more varied – censuses, deeds, ecclesiastical archives, tax lists and trade directories – and the archaeological stratigraphy is more complex and material culture much richer. A brief perusal of the post-medieval archaeologies of the great towns and cities of Europe, where urban archaeology has a significant history, illustrates the knowledge gains to be made. Urban sites were also the places where a number of different ethnic groups worked out their daily lives, and some of the latter have left little written trace. The Archaeology in Annapolis (Maryland) project began in 1981 and from the outset attempted to give a voice to the poorest of the urban population – the working class and the African-Americans.

▲ A *Nkisi* from an excavated house in Annapolis, Maryland. The special collection of objects covered by part of a pearl-ware bowl suggests the presence of slaves of African descent practising divination ceremonies.

> Archaeology in Annapolis designed a two-step process that sought to (1) uncover contemporary inequalities in daily life, and (2) utilize public archaeology as a means of presenting the idea that these inequalities were not inevitable ...
>
> *www.aia.umd.edu*

One example of the dispossessed speaking was the discovery of pearl-ware bowl placed face down, covering crystals, pieces of chipped quartz, a faceted glass bead, and a polished black stone. These dated to around 1800 CE and were located in quarters occupied by African and African-American slaves. The artefacts proved to be a ritual collection comprising a Nkisi, used in divination ceremonies in West Africa. Such facets of urban lives were never likely to be recorded in official documents.

Maritime archaeology

Maritime archaeology, and particularly that aspect of it associated with shipwrecks, has a pivotal role to play in amplifying and in some cases contradicting associated documentary evidence. A shipwreck was clearly a catastrophic event but its value to the archaeological record lies in the fact that it comprises material culture sunk and sealed at a specific moment in time – an underwater time capsule.

Time and time again official records of ships tell one story of their crew and inventories, while archaeology paints a very different picture as individual captains made unrecorded decisions and crewmen engaged in a wide variety of unauthorized activities. A sunken ship, a lost cargo, and a drowned crew with their personal possessions also constitute an intensely moving and personal window into the past. Henry VIII's flagship, the *Mary Rose,* sank in the Solent in 1545 in full view of the king himself. Approximately 19,000 artefacts have been excavated, many of which belonged to the 400 or so crew who were in their late teens or early twenties. A rather well-off member on-board was probably a carpenter. One cabin on the ship contained a range of tools for carpentry, including a mallet, brace, planes, rulers and a mortise gauge. The carpenter also kept his prized pewter safely locked away in a chest, along with silver coins and jewelry, a book, an embroidered leather pouch and a sundial in an embossed leather case. It is such personal possessions of crew members that escaped record in standard inventories.

Landscapes and townscapes provide rich repositories for collective and individual memories in the historical period. So much so, that at times those in power seek to erase those memories by deliberate acts of destruction. Agents of Henry VIII during the English Reformation sought to eradicate the presence of the Catholic Church through organized destruction of the monasteries; stripping parish churches of statuary and white-washing their walls. They hoped that by destroying the material traces of the Catholic Church they would loosen its hold on the population. In District Six of Cape Town the Apartheid regime sought to establish white ownership in new townhouses and high-rise flats. Its mostly 'coloured' inhabitants were forcibly removed and their buildings flattened in an attempt to render the past forgotten. However, the dispossessed did not forget and once the Apartheid administration fell the former inhabitants reclaimed their urban landscape and memorialized it in the new District Six Museum.

The historical associations of individual monuments in the landscape can be manipulated over time. In Vorpommern (Germany) a monument was erected in 1924, commemorating the dead of a local regiment. A chain erected at its entrance reminded everyone of the humiliated Germany after the treaty of Versailles 'As you step over these chains remember the fatherland's honour and freedom must be reinstated'. When Hitler came to power the chains were broken in a symbolic act of resurgence. After 1946, with the war lost, the monument was a source of shame, its national symbols removed, and forgotten. It re-opened in 1995 – re-dedicated and re-appreciated in the light of Germany's reunification.

A special focus for historical archaeology is the study of standing buildings, particularly vernacular architecture in the countryside as opposed to its 'polite' counterpart in the towns. Historic buildings can be studied from a wide range of sources, but principally cartographic information, probate inventories of former occupants, census and taxation records and the physical structure of the building itself. Forms of vernacular architecture vary from region to region, depending on the availability of raw building materials, climate, local traditions of construction and the social and residential requirements of the building. Examples of vernacular buildings, many still standing, have usually been modified a number of times and it is this disentangling of modifications and adaptations that challenge the archaeologist. In some ways the archaeological task is more difficult than in traditional 'below-ground' archaeology. With the latter, by and large, the deeper you dig, the older the deposits. With standing buildings the older elements could be the foundations, or the timbers of the roof structure. In addition there is the frequent re-use of materials. Old timbers from one part of the house could have been reworked and used in a more recent modification. The archaeology of standing buildings is a three-dimensional stratigraphic puzzle.

▶ Contemporary archaeology

Having read the above, you might now be convinced that, even in those countries with an abundance of surviving historical documentation, archaeology still has a role to play fleshing out those silences and glosses in the written evidence. But when does archaeology stop? Is there a period when archaeological investigation ceases to have any relevance? Surely in the age of social networking, super-power and corporate surveillance of our digital lives, in a period where it seems almost everyone has a mobile phone and camera, then the word and image hold centre stage and archaeological methodologies have become redundant? And the idea that archaeology in the present can have any conceivable role for the future is, well, just inconceivable.

Perhaps, but then maybe not. If we hold to the idea that the goal of archaeology is to reveal through material culture interpretations of the lives of others then our digitally generated records can only take us so far. Let me provide you with one example which wasn't even conceived of as an archaeological project but which provided data on a contemporary lifestyle activity that would not have been recoverable from any documentary evidence.

Governments are naturally always interested in taxes. In the UK, a long-standing source of taxable income is that derived from sales of cigarettes, so it was of interest to the UK tax authorities to estimate how much tax avoidance was associated with tobacco consumption. Between 2008 and 2013 a consultancy firm was appointed to investigate this issue. The firm obviously decided that since fraudulent activities were not likely to be recorded in official documents a more innovative, indeed archaeological, approach was required. So they conducted surveys in 100 towns across the UK collecting discarded cigarette packets from pavements and litter bins categorizing them as either duty-paid or duty-avoided. A quantitative analysis of the results indicated that the town of Gillingham, in south-east England, was the worst offender. Towns with the highest number of illicit smokes were Gillingham, with 54.5 per cent, Poole at 50.83 per cent and Worthing with 49.24 per cent. The authorities then moved on to an essentially archaeological interpretation. They suggested that Gillingham was the offender probably because of its proximity to the Channel ports – and Europe from where the illicit goods came.

So what are the other areas of the contemporary world in which archaeologists find themselves involved? One very up to date application is that of forensic archaeology. Police forces, unfortunately, are quite often called upon to locate and excavate burials – the result of contemporary criminal activity. They increasingly turn to archaeologists, who for generations have become quite sophisticated in their examination of the deceased of more remote periods. Forensic archaeology is thus the application of archaeological mapping and excavation skills to death scenes or places where bodies have been recently disposed or buried. In forensic work, archaeologists need a strong sense of detachment, and the ability to present evidence clearly in court.

The archaeology of modern conflict is another specialist niche that has emerged in the last few decades. The discovery of a Second World War U-boat off the coast of New Jersey hundreds of miles from any reported U-boat contact sparked a detailed historical and archaeological project that eventually identified the vessel as U-869, captained by Hellmut Neuerburg. The human remains still in the U-boat raised ethical concerns about the investigation. However, the identification of the submarine allowed the final resting place of the crew to be definitively known and wreaths were laid on the wreck by divers. The First World War trenches in Flanders have been the location of several archaeological projects. One such investigated the trench system that underlay the site of the 1917 Battle of Messines. Under the cratered battlefield the body of an infantry man, face down, in full kit was located. Careful examination of the soldier's personal items allowed him to be identified first as an Australian and subsequently as a specific individual. Individuality, remembrance and commemoration were thus restored to one of the thousands who died without record.

When does an object become an archaeological object? In the case of the Tucson Garbage Project, started in 1973 and led by Professor William Rathje for over two decades, the answer is as soon as it is discarded. Garbology, as it is now known, is the science of examining the waste that you and I throw away. You might think that we know all there is to know about what we discard, but Rathje demonstrated that we cannot be trusted to tell others the truth. His students studied the contents of Tucson residents' waste in order to examine patterns of consumption. Quantitative data from bins was compared with information known about the residents who owned them. The results demonstrated that information people freely volunteered about their consumption habits did not always tally with the contents of their waste bins. For example, alcohol consumption was proven to be significantly higher in reality than in the questionnaires completed by the people studied. Such findings highlighted the difference between people's self-reported and actual behaviours. They also suggest that such biases frequently were present in much older documentary evidence, although these are much more difficult to detect now.

The archaeology of space

For the budding archaeologist mapping out a potential career, outer space could be the place to look. The archaeology of space exploration – defined as relevant material culture either on Earth or in outer space – can only get bigger. There is a growing density of space junk orbiting the Earth. Estimates suggest that there are over 19,000 pieces whose largest dimension is greater than 100mm tracking in Earth Orbit. There are satellites that are already heritage assets. Vanguard 1 – launched by the USA in 1958 and the oldest human object in orbit – is predicted to remain circling the Earth every two hours for the next 600 years. Future generations of space tourists will no doubt find this a standard stop on any excursion.

Tranquility Base, the first lunar site with human activity, is unique. The human footprints made in moon dust are reminiscent of those made by ancient hominin feet in the volcanic ash of Laetoli (Tanzania), some 3.6 million years ago. But you can forget dreaming of being the first person to survey an 'ancient monument' on the moon. It has already been done by a couple of Apollo 12 astronauts in 1969 who recorded the condition of an un-manned probe that had soft-landed some three years earlier.

The archaeology of the contemporary also becomes tangled up from time to time with modern politics. A couple of examples suffice. Kennewick Man is the name for the skeletal remains of a prehistoric man found on a bank of the Columbia River in Kennewick, Washington, USA, on 28 July 1996. It was one of the most complete skeletons ever found in North America. A stone projectile point was found in the man's hip bone, while dating tests indicated an approximate age of between 7600 and 7300 BCE. The discovery, however, triggered an acrimonious and legally controversial nine-year debate between Native American tribes who claimed Kennewick Man as one of their ancestors, and archaeologists and scientists who wished to study the remains. Ultimately the Circuit Court Magistrate ruled that the remains did not fit the definition of Native American defined in current legislation and thus the scientists were able to study Kennewick Man. This judicial decision widens the gulf between Archaeologists and American Indians, fuelling the debate over who owns and controls the past. In addition it raises the thorny issue of the specific moment in time when cultures 'became' Native American.

In Europe controversy periodically erupts around the fate of the Elgin Marbles, a frieze of sculptures currently in the British Museum but formerly decorating the most famous ancient Greek temple on the Acropolis in Athens – the Parthenon. A spat occurred over the Marbles, for example, in 2014 between actor George Clooney, who favoured their return to Greece, and the Mayor of London, who didn't. A new Acropolis Museum currently within sight of the Parthenon has also led to increased calls for their return to the Greek capital.

The growth of Community Archaeology projects, involving people who live locally, will not solve some of these historic entanglements, but may help to prevent their re-occurrence. In Australia some indigenous groups now manage their own heritage resources, and archaeologists are employed by local communities. A substantive shift in attitudes now sees archaeological involvement with indigenous peoples as a privilege rather than a right.

Contemporary archaeology has a role in deciding what heritage resources survive for the future. The time between a building or an object becoming 'archaeology' and the time when purposeful decisions are taken to record or preserve either or both for future generations as 'heritage' will inevitably shrink. Recall Luke Skywalker:

> As I researched further I found it was not uncommon for Hollywood and European productions to abandon sets in deserts. In Morocco there are huge recreations of ancient Rome and Greece, plus a fake Mecca ... Over time they become almost like archaeological sites.
>
> *Rä di Martino*

The Berlin Wall fell in November 1989 and, through the rightful outpouring of the populace in both East and West Germany, it was torn down. Today very little of the original Wall survives. Future generations may regret the extensive obliteration of the detested barrier. More sections of it could have remained as a reminder of the value of freedom and the struggle for liberty and German reunification. A survey of Russians in 2011 indicated that already some 58 per cent of the population did not know who had built the Berlin Wall. And sadly and more hazardously archaeologists also find themselves increasingly involved in war-zones – implementing heritage salvage procedures in places like Afghanistan, Iraq and Syria.

▲ The East Side Gallery is an international memorial for freedom. It is a 1.3 km long section of the Berlin Wall located on Mühlenstraße in Friedrichshain-Kreuzberg. The Gallery includes 105 paintings by artists from all over the world, painted in 1990 on the east side of the Wall.

▶ Postscript

The first part of this small book outlined the techniques and practices of archaeology. The second half examined archaeologists' discoveries, particularly in relation to types of societies that have been labelled 'band 'or 'tribe' or 'chiefdom' or 'state', or societies in historical periods.

As an archaeologist I don't think you can really understand ancient buildings, tombs and artefacts without some idea of the people and society that created them – how they organized themselves socially, economically and politically, and what they believed in. Ancient people are the key to a fuller understanding of the human past, but it's the challenge of archaeology, and also the source of its excitement, that we have to develop that understanding from the material that those people left behind.

It is important to reiterate also that these labels – band – tribe – chiefdom – state – do not constitute an evolutionary sequence, from simple to complex. So should we just abandon this quadripartite division? I think eventually this four-fold classification will disappear, no doubt to be replaced by much more numerous and complex sets of criteria for different types of social organization. The organizational reality of the human past, however, is more likely to be one of almost infinite variety than closely defined categories, no matter how numerous. Ethnographic evidence suggests that societies without permanent leaders can function well enough, and fixed hierarchies are not a pre-requisite of political stability. The discoveries of decorated stone monoliths at Göbekli Tepe in south-eastern Turkey since the mid-1990s, apparently sanctuaries dating from the 10th millennium BCE and erected by communities who still lived by hunting and gathering, demonstrate clearly that a vast range of very different communities can be lumped unhelpfully together if all are described simply as 'hunting bands'.

▲ Göbekli Tepe includes two main phases of ritual use dating back to the 10th–8th millennium BCE. During the first phase, circles of massive T-shaped stone pillars were erected, some of them decorated. The site may have functioned as a centre of ritual and pilgrimage for people who still lived by hunting and gathering.

Let's end on a human note. Archaeologists sometimes write as if communities and societies were monolithic blocks, expanding or fissuring with a collective mindset and resolve. Catastrophic causes, acting alone or in combination, such as climate change, warfare, declining access to prestige goods, changes in beliefs, disease, over-population, diminishing resources, are invoked as the drivers of such change. But many of the social changes that archaeology seeks to uncover took place over a much lengthier timescale than a single human life. After all, I doubt that many people around the western Mediterranean in the early 5th century CE appreciated they were living during the disintegration of the Western Roman Empire. Nor can those hard-pressed gatherers who planted the first seeds of cultivation at various places around the globe some 10,000 years ago have speculated that they were possibly the pioneers in a food-production revolution that still reverberates today.

The changes that drove differences in the way human groups organized themselves stemmed from myriad uncoordinated and incremental decisions taken by individuals. These decisions had intended or unintended effects that were sometimes adopted as social norms by most members of a single community, and occasionally manipulated by those who sought greater status than others. These innumerable decisions that helped guide the history of humanity make for very tangled webs indeed. It is the job of archaeologists, sometimes assisted by other professions, to do the untangling. And if that seems like a very big challenge indeed, well, you can give your support or even lend a hand! In the '100 Ideas' section that follows you will find out how.

This 100 ideas section gives ways you can explore the subject in more depth. It's much more than just the usual reading list, with some stemming from the world's greatest archaeological discoveries – and the world's greatest archaeologists!

100 IDEAS

A highly selective list of ten great archaeologists to fire the imagination!

1   Kathleen Kenyon One of the great women archaeologists of the 20th century, most famous for her careful excavation of the ancient city of Jericho.

2   The Leakey family: Mary, Louis and Richard. This family of archaeologists and anthropologists made huge strides

in our understanding of the development of early hominins in Africa, particularly through work in the Olduvai Gorge (Tanzania).

3 **Sir Arthur Evans** Discovered and excavated the Palace of Minos at Knossos on the island of Crete. Not everyone agrees with his controversial reconstruction of the site though!

4 **Jacques Cousteau** Inventor of the aqualung which enabled underwater divers to develop more rigorous methods of recording shipwrecks; he was a pioneer of marine archaeology.

5 **Boucher de Perthes** The French geologist Jacques Boucher de Crevecour de Perthes was born in 1788 and was noted for being one of the first academics to form the idea that an archaeological chronology could be charted using periods of geological time.

6 **Mortimer Wheeler** Scottish archaeologist who worked on several significant UK sites such as Verulamium (St Albans) and Maiden Castle (Dorset), and who founded the Indian Archaeological Survey.

7 **OGS Crawford** The founder of aerial photography for archaeological research. His main contribution was in the methods that he developed for producing and analysing the results of photographically acquired archaeological data.

8 **Alfred Kroeber** Although he is known primarily as a cultural anthropologist, he did significant work in archaeology and anthropological linguistics, conducting excavations in New Mexico, Mexico, and Peru.

9 **Colin Renfrew** Famous for his work on the application of radiocarbon dating to archaeology, as well as his political attempts to prevent the sale of looted archaeological objects as art-works.

10 Howard Carter An English archaeologist and Egyptologist who became world famous after discovering the intact tomb of 14th-century BCE pharaoh Tutankhamun (colloquially known as 'King Tut' and 'the boy king').

Ten of the greatest archaeological finds

11 The Dead Sea Scrolls A collection of 972 texts discovered between 1946 and 1956 at Khirbet Qumran in the West Bank (modern Israel). They were found near the Dead Sea, hence their name, and 40 per cent of them are copies of text from the Hebrew Bible. The biblical manuscripts in the Scrolls push back documentary evidence for the Bible until the 2nd century BCE.

12 The Rosetta Stone Crucial for the decipherment of hieroglyphs, the inscription on the Rosetta Stone is a decree passed by a council of priests in 196 BCE on behalf of King Ptolemy V. It appears in three scripts: the upper text is Ancient Egyptian hieroglyphs, the middle portion Demotic script, and lowest Ancient Greek.

13 The Sutton Hoo helmet Found in an Anglo-Saxon ship burial in East Anglia (UK), this dates from the early 7th century CE. This extraordinary helmet is very rare.

14 The Grauballe Man A bog body that was uncovered in 1952 from a peat bog near to the village of Grauballe in Jutland, Denmark. The body is that of a man dating from the late 3rd century BCE. Based on the evidence of his wounds, he was most likely killed by having his throat slit open. His corpse was then deposited in the bog, where his body was naturally preserved for over two millennia. Such ritual sacrifices appear to be widespread in the Iron Age of northern Europe.

15 Tutankhamun An Egyptian pharaoh of the 18th dynasty (who ruled *c.* 1332–1323 BCE), during the period of Egyptian history known as the New Kingdom. His tomb, and the pharaoh's iconic death-mask, was discovered in 1922 by Howard Carter.

16 The Venus of Willendorf Now known more correctly as the Woman of Willendorf, is a 10.8 cm high statuette of a female figure estimated to have been carved between about 28,000 and 25,000 BCE. It was found in 1908 at an Upper Palaeolithic site near Willendorf, a village in Lower Austria.

17 Bronze objects found in 1986 in the second sacrificial pit at Sanxingdui, Sichuan, China These included male sculptures, animal-faced sculptures, bells, decorative animals such as dragons, snakes, chicks, and birds, and axes. Tables, masks and belts were some of the objects found made out of gold while objects made out of jade included axes, tablets, rings, knives and tubes. They date from the 12th to 11th centuries BCE.

18 Stone statue of the Mayan maize god Found in a pyramid-style temple in Copan in modern-day Honduras surrounded by many other maize gods. It was probably carved around 700 CE. In Mayan mythology, the maize god was decapitated at harvest time but reborn again at the beginning of a new growing season.

19 Wooden Sudanese slit drum This became a pivotal artefact in British-Sudanese colonial relations. The buffalo-shaped drum once played in an indigenous court orchestra and was used to transmit messages or summon warriors to war. The drum was captured by the British and Egyptian army at the Battle of Omdurman, near Khartoum, in 1898 and presented to Queen Victoria by Lord Kitchener. Perhaps not strictly an archaeological find, but this example demonstrates the powerful symbolism of certain artefacts.

20 Pottery vessels crafted in Ancient Japan during the Jōmon period These are generally accepted to be the oldest pottery in Japan. Some date from as early as 10,500 BCE. The majority of Jōmon pottery has rounded bottoms and the vessels are typically small. This shows that the vessels would probably be used to boil food, perhaps sitting in a fire.

Ten of the greatest archaeological sites yet uncovered

If you are not moved by a visit to any one of these then archaeology is not for you!

21 Pompeii and Herculaneum Two great Roman cities in the bay of Naples, buried by the eruption of Vesuvius in 79 CE.

22 Cave of Altamira In northern Spain, the cave contains breathtaking Upper Palaeolithic paintings of wild mammals and human hands.

23 Teotihuacan A 2000-year-old city 50 km north-east of Mexico City. It is famed as the site of many of the most architecturally significant Mesoamerican pyramids built in the pre-Columbian Americas.

24 Angkor Wat First a Hindu, then subsequently a Buddhist temple complex in Cambodia and the largest religious monument in the world. The temple was built by the Khmer King Suryavarman II in the early 12th century CE in the capital of the Khmer Empire, as his state temple and eventual mausoleum.

100 Ideas

25 Olduvai Gorge Lies in Tanzania and is a steep-sided ravine in the Great Rift Valley that stretches through eastern Africa. The site was occupied by *Homo habilis* approximately 1.9 million years ago, *Paranthropus boisei* 1.8 million years ago, and *Homo erectus* 1.2 million years ago.

26 Terracotta Army Buried with Qin Shi Huang, the first Emperor of China in 210–209 BCE near Xi'an, China. The soldiers are a form of funerary art whose purpose was to protect the emperor in his afterlife.

27 Machu Picchu A 15th-century CE Inca site located in the Andes at an altitude of some 2,430 metres above sea-level near Cusco, Peru. Most archaeologists believe that Machu Picchu was built as an estate for the Inca emperor Pachacuti (1438–1472).

28 Mohenjo-Daro An urban site built around the middle of the 3rd millennium BCE in southern Pakistan. Forms a type-site for the so-called Indus Valley Civilization. Part-excavated by Mortimer Wheeler.

29 Great Zimbabwe A monumental ruined city in the south-eastern hills of Zimbabwe. Built by ancestors of the Shona people between the 11th and 14th centuries CE. For a long time in the 20th century political pressure was exerted on the archaeological establishment to suggest it was the work of non-indigenous non-black people.

30 Rapa Nui statues The Moai (stone statues) built by the Rapa Nui, the inhabitants of Easter Island, between 1250 and 1500 CE. There are 887 statues, believed to be the faces of living ancestors, set up on stone altars, many on the coastal perimeters of the island.

Bad ideas! Top ten archaeological hoaxes

31 The Piltdown Man A hoax in which bone fragments were presented as the fossilized remains of a previously unknown early human. These fragments consisted of parts of a skull and jawbone, said to have been collected in 1912 from a gravel pit at Piltdown, East Sussex, England.

32 The crystal skulls Human skull carvings made of clear or milky white quartz, known in art history as 'rock crystal', claimed to be pre-Columbian Mesoamerican artefacts by their alleged finders; however, none of the specimens made available for scientific study have been authenticated as pre-Columbian in origin.

33 Saitaphernes' Golden Tiara On April 1, 1896, the Louvre in Paris announced that it had purchased a gold tiara that had belonged to the Scythian king, Saitaphernes. The museum had purchased the artefact for 200,000 gold French francs. To the experts at the Louvre, an inscription on the tiara confirmed an episode dating to the late 3rd century BCE or early 2nd century BCE. A skilled goldsmith had, however, fashioned the tiara in 1894.

34 Fawcett's deadly idol The 10-inch tall basalt figure, known as Fawcett's deadly idol, was given to British explorer Percy Fawcett by H. Rider Haggard, author of such novels about ancient treasures and lost races as *King Solomon's Mines* (1885) and *She* (1887). Haggard 'obtained it from Brazil, and [I] ... believed that it came from one of the lost cities'. However and wherever Haggard obtained the object, it was a fake. Fawcett believed in the idol, carrying it into the Brazilian jungle in 1925 in a search for lost cities. He never returned.

35 *Chariots of the Gods?*, written by Erich von Däniken, was first published in 1968. It became an international bestseller. The thesis of the book was that ancient human civilizations had contact with visitors from outer space. These 'ancient astronauts' were supposedly responsible for many of the great architectural feats of history, such as the Egyptian pyramids, the Nazca lines of Peru, and the statue on Rapa Nui. Suffice to say no supporting evidence for this thesis has ever been found.

36 The city of Veleia Situated in northern Spain, the city was settled in the Bronze Age, around 1000 BCE. During the first two centuries CE, it expanded into a Roman city. Remarkable graffiti found on pottery sherds in 2005 and 2006 were initially thought to be genuine, but are now regarded by most experts as fakes.

37 The Stone Age discoveries of Shinichi Fujimura On October 22 in 2000 Shinichi Fujimura and his team announced the discovery in Japan of a cluster of stone pieces they believed to be the work of primitive people. They also found several holes that, they hypothesized, had held pillars supporting primitive dwellings. The stones and holes were believed to be over 600,000 years old, making them one of the oldest signs of human habitation in the world. For this reason, the discovery drew international attention. But on November 5 the *Mainichi Shimbun* published three pictures on its front page showing Fujimura digging holes at the site and burying artefacts he later dug up and announced as major finds.

38 The Kinderhook Plates These were an archaeological hoax designed to embarrass the Mormons by tricking their leader, Joseph Smith, into translating phony hieroglyphics written on them. The plates were six bell-shaped pieces of flat copper, unearthed from an Indian burial mound near Kinderhook, Illinois in April 1843. The hieroglyphics were inscribed on the front of the plates. The plates were supposedly found buried beside the skeleton of a man. The hoax was later revealed to be the work of three men – Wilbur Fugate, Robert Wiley, and Bridge Whitton – who lived near Kinderhook.

39 The Calaveras Skull A human skull found by miners in Calaveras County, California which was purported to prove that humans, mastodons, and elephants had coexisted in California. It was later revealed to be a hoax. Coincidentally, 'calaveras' is the Spanish word for 'skulls'.

40 The Etruscan terracotta warriors Three statues that resemble the work of the ancient Etruscans, but are in fact art forgeries. The statues, created by Italian brothers Pio and Alfonso Riccardi and three of their six sons, were bought by the New York Metropolitan Museum of Art between 1915 and 1921. They were conclusively shown to be forgeries in 1961.

Ten of the greatest fictional archaeologists – dream on!

(Archaeologists portrayed by writers of fiction reflect some well-known stereotypes – the action hero, the brainy academic or the eccentric scholar who is lost in the 'real world'.)

41 Dr Henry Walton 'Indiana' Jones Jr Particularly notable facets of the character include his iconic look (bullwhip, fedora, and leather jacket), sense of humour, deep knowledge of many ancient civilizations and languages, and fear of snakes.

42 Lara Croft A fictional character and the protagonist of the video game series *Tomb Raider*. She is presented as a beautiful, intelligent, and athletic English archaeologist-adventurer who ventures into ancient, hazardous tombs and ruins around the world.

43 Benjamin Gates In the film *National Treasure* he famously styled himself a 'treasure protector' to differentiate himself from the Indiana Jones franchise. Gates fumbles his way from one treasure to the next using clues spelled out to him in advance with unusual clarity and timing!

44 *Bonekickers* A BBC drama about a team of archaeologists, set at the fictional Wessex University in the UK. It included an element of science mixed with conspiracy theories. Although real-life archaeologist Mark Horton acted as a consultant, the reviews were poor and the BBC did not commission a second series.

45 *Babylon 5* In this film Garibaldi returns to confer with archaeologist Dr. Robert Bryson, who claims to be on the verge of discovering the secret of eternal life. Alas, the immortality-granting alien artefact discovered by Bryson actually belongs to the Soul Hunters, who will stop at nothing to retrieve the sacred relic. Trouble ahead!

46 *The Mummy* In this film an English archaeologist/librarian called Evelyn 'Evy' Carnahan wants to start an archaeological dig at the ancient city of Hamunaptra, with the help of adventurer Rick O'Connell, after rescuing him from prison. A stiff-limbed heavily-bandaged actor, aka the Mummy, inevitably causes the subsequent mayhem!

47 *Hi-de-Hi!* In this famous British sitcom of the 1980s set in a holiday camp, Jeffrey Fairbrother, a Professor of Archaeology at Cambridge University, resigned his academic post and joined Maplins Holiday Camp in 1959 as Entertainment Manager, in the fictional seaside town of Crimpton on Sea, Essex. An unlikely plot but in real-life archaeology is full of surprises!

48 River Song An archaeologist from the future who keeps getting into trouble and knows Doctor Who can help her get out of it. She first meets the Doctor on the planet of The Library and her journal is packed with information the Doctor feels he should not know about yet.

49 *Star Trek* Captain Jean-Luc Picard (played by Patrick Stewart) is the Commander of the United Federation of Planet's flagship, the USS Enterprise, who served during the latter half of the 24th century. Jean-Luc's interest in history and archaeology began in 2313, when he entered a small parish church to escape the torment of his brother.

50 Dr Daniel Jackson Played by James Spader in the 1994 film *Stargate*, in which a small group of US troops use an ancient alien 'stargate' device to transport themselves to a distant planet called Abydos, after Jackson uses his knowledge of ancient Egyptian languages to make the device work.

Ten of the best archaeological websites from around the world

51 http://www.culture.gouv.fr/culture/arcnat/chauvet/en/ These pages present some of the images of the Palaeolithic cave paintings found in 1994, at Vallon-Pont d'Arc in the Ardèche region of France. The illustrations are accompanied by text which describes the paintings' subject matter, significance, dating and other related matters of interest.

52 https://pantherfile.uwm.edu/barnold/www/arch/arch.html A Landscape of Ancestors: The Heuneburg Archaeological Project. This site represents a long-term research project involving excavations in an early Iron Age archaeological landscape in south-western Germany. The project focuses on a group of burial mounds or tumuli associated with one of the best excavated and most extensively studied late Hallstatt period (600–400 BCE) hillfort settlements in western Europe

53 http://oi.uchicago.edu/ The Oriental Institute is a research organization and museum devoted to the study of the ancient Near East. Founded in 1919 by James Henry Breasted, the Institute, a part of the University of Chicago, is an internationally recognized pioneer in the archaeology, philology, and history of early Near Eastern civilizations.

54 http://www.archeurope.com/ A comprehensive website for Europe providing information on many archaeological subjects, archaeological events such as study tours, field trips and archaeological courses, links to other websites and articles and lists of favourite archaeological sites.

55 http://www.archaeological.org/ One of the premier websites emanating from North America. The Archaeological Institute of America (AIA) promotes archaeological inquiry and public understanding of the material record of the human past to foster an appreciation of diverse cultures and our shared humanity. A fantastic resource and a great organization!

56 http://archaeology.about.com/ Another portal site that is a real Pandora's Box! Deals with archaeology around the world and contains extensive information including how much money you can expect to earn as an archaeologist.

57 http://www.china.org.cn/english/features/Archaeology/93066.htm An official Chinese website that pulls together a lot of information on the archaeology of China: from a general survey of Chinese archaeology, to a list of the year's top discoveries and a section on ancient pagodas.

58 http://whc.unesco.org/ The United Nations Educational, Scientific and Cultural Organization (UNESCO) seeks to encourage the identification, protection and preservation of cultural and natural heritage around the world considered to be of outstanding value to humanity. You can catch up on progress to date by consulting this impressive website.

59 http://www.australianarchaeologicalassociation.com.au/ The Australian Archaeological Association Inc. (AAA) is the largest archaeological organization in Australia, representing a diverse membership of professionals, students and others with an interest in archaeology. AAA aims to promote the advancement of archaeology; to provide an organization for the discussion and dissemination of archaeological information and ideas.

60 http://www.african-archaeology.net/index.html An indispensable introduction to the archaeology of Africa, including thematic articles, available databases, institutions working in Africa and field data by region. Not the prettiest of websites but it's the content that counts!

Ten things to take, remember or say when you go on your first dig ...

61 A GPS device, or failing that a compass It's always useful to know where Magnetic North is and the site director and supervisors will no doubt pepper their guided site tours with reference to the cardinal points.

62 Basic terminology Know the local geology in basic terms – i.e. is it sand, gravel, clay or stone, and if the latter, what sort of stone?

63 A pointed trowel A WHS 4-inch pointing trowel used to be gold standard in the UK, but there are other makes around. Plus perhaps one or two small paint brushes for any delicate work, like removing soil from *in situ* bones.

64 Hand-tape and digital camera Another must is a 5-m hand-tape, one that can fit snugly on your belt, and a small digital camera. Even if you are never asked to take an official record photograph or measure anything that matters, you will look the part!

65 A notebook Hard-back with lined paper on one side and metric graph paper on the other. Record your experiences day by day, and do the odd sketch, more or less to scale, of parts of the trench you are working on.

66 **A plastic tool box** This can serve as a great container for some of the above, but if it's your first week or day on site you might not want to cut such a know-it-all figure until you get to know your rooky colleagues better!

67 **Key questions** Learn some key questions to ask the supervisors, such as 'I think there might be a feature here, the soil feels slightly different. What do you think?' You may not know what sort of feature it is, but successful excavation relies on being able to spot features early, so the fact that you might be looking for one will earn you brownie points!

68 **pH of the soil** Another thing either to find out or remember is the pH of the local soil – basically whether it is acidic or alkaline. If it's the latter then bones and shells will survive, if it's the former – then they won't.

69 **Safety footwear** All diggers, novices and experienced alike, must wear safety footwear – which usually means hard toe-capped safety boots. Carelessly slung pick-axes and mattocks can do awful damage to shins and feet!

70 **Fit and ready to go** Before you go, get down to the gym and muscle up! Seriously, digging all day five or six days a week can be quite strenuous. You need to be as physically fit and supple as you can. So work out a training programme to suit you!

Ten ways you can get involved with your local archaeology

71 **Visit your nearest museum** This should tell you something about the history and archaeology of your area, and the kind of objects that are particular to your village, town or region.

72 **Dig that hole in your garden** As described at the start of this book, dig yourself a hole in your garden and examine the artefacts you find. How did they come to be there? What was their function?

73 **Join your local archaeological society** It may be a little daunting at first, especially if you are new to archaeology, but persevere!

74 **Magazines and journals** Wherever you live there are probably archaeology magazines that you could subscribe to. *Current Archaeology* and *British Archaeology* are two well-known ones in the UK and bring news of the latest discoveries. *Archaeology*, the magazine of the Archaeological Institute of America, contains news of the latest discoveries worldwide.

75 **Watch TV** Trawl through the TV stations and watch some archaeological documentaries – but don't believe everything they tell you – a sceptical outlook is useful sometimes.

76 **Visit the library** Pop into your nearest library and see what archaeology books it has on the shelves. Read those that either look interesting or are most recently published.

77 **Go to talks** Your local society or museum or adult education provider probably organizes archaeological walk and talks from time to time – see if there are any that interest you.

78 **On your doorstep** Have a look around at your own house, street, village and town. How did it develop? Where are the oldest buildings and streets? What materials are the buildings made from? Do they have any specific features peculiar to the locality or region?

79 **Historic records** Try and visit the public institution that holds the historic records for your village or region. Most such institutions have introductory courses or sessions on the range of local history records they hold. So take one of these courses first – it will all make much more sense if you do!

80 **Look on a map** Get a detailed map of your immediate locality – whether urban or rural – and start to investigate the street names or place-names you find. Why is that street called so-and-so street, or where did that farm get its name? Asking these sorts of questions will have you trawling the web for the meanings of place-names and borrowing books on place-names from your library. Names of buildings, farms, fields or streets are usually linked to some aspect of the past, so finding out their meaning will tell you something of the history of your own locality.

Ten of the best board and video games in archaeology – but don't take them too seriously!

81 **Roman Town** Allows users to excavate archaeological sites. The video game is geared towards children and teaches Roman history through archaeology.

82 **Tomb Raider** Lara Croft is an archaeologist gone bad, raiding tombs for her own profit and gain. The very thought of what she does is enough to make an archaeologist foam at the mouth!

83 **Indiana Jones** The films have spawned a number of video games but everyone's favourite seems to be the LEGO video games. They include all the kitsch and homage for the original movies you could want with a combination of combat and puzzles.

84 **Borderlands** This gets an honourable mention in the video game category. The plot has some archaeological threads about unearthing alien artefacts and ruins as well as being able to find artefacts along the way.

85 Dust More of an anthropological exercise but those interested in ancient civilizations will enjoy this unique take on video gaming. The game allows you to manipulate an island landscape in order to progress the civilization of a nomadic tribe.

86 Archaeology: The Card Game This game is for those who shun the hi-tech and want to keep life simple. You are an archaeologist, albeit a very mercenary one, working on the archaeological sites of the Egyptian desert. Search for the right pieces to complete torn parchments, broken pots and other priceless artefacts.

87 Barrow Hill: Curse of the Ancient Circle A video game ... with a little archaeology in it. Barrow Hill is a mystery/adventure game in the same style of the all-time classic *Myst*. It takes a first person perspective as you point and click your way through an abandoned service station, woods and swamp while trying to solve the mystery surrounding the nearby ancient stone circle.

88 Thebes A board game of competitive archaeology. Players are archaeologists who must travel around Europe, northern Africa, and the Middle East to acquire knowledge about five ancient civilizations – the Greeks, the Cretans, the Egyptians, the Palestinians, and the Mesopotamians.

89 Mykerinos Board game in which archaeologists seek relics from ancient Egypt in order to win favour from powerful benefactors.

90 Pergamon Tactical collecting board game with a theme based on excavating archaeological discoveries and managing their exhibition. Set in the year 1878, the first excavations in what is now modern Turkey are uncovering the remains of ancient Pergamon.

Ten theories on the function and meaning of Stonehenge

These are very roughly listed from plausible (top) to extremely unlikely (bottom). You can continue this list by adding your own theories at the bottom – chances are, your ideas will be as thought-provoking as anyone else's!

91 It was a pilgrimage centre to which people came for cures, rather like present-day Lourdes.

92 It was a site for commemorating the dead.

93 It was built to celebrate the winter solstice and bring people together.

94 It was a computer for predicting astronomical events.

95 It was the centre of Druidic culture that had sophisticated, but oral, knowledge.

96 It was built by the Phoenicians who came in search of gold, tin and copper.

97 It was a venue for Neolithic raves, since the stones have acoustic properties that amplify a repetitive trance rhythm.

98 It was a giant fertility symbol, constructed in the shape of a vulva, to represent Mother Earth.

99 It was a spaceport for extra-terrestrials, since it could not have been built solely by humans.

100 It was built by the wizard Merlin as a burial place for Knights slain fighting the Saxons.

Further reading

There is a comprehensive literature on Archaeology, and the small selection below provides a sample.

Bahn, P, ed., 2014, *The History of Archaeology*, Oxon: Routledge

Barker, G, 2009. Early Farming and Domestication, in Cunliffe *et al*, *The Oxford Book of Archaeology*, 445–483.

Bintliff, J, & Pearce, JM, eds. 2011. *The Death of Archaeological Theory?* Oxford: Oxbow Books.

Cunliffe, B, Gosden, C, & Joyce, RA, eds. 2009. *The Oxford Handbook of Archaeology*. Oxford: Oxford University Press.

Drewett, PL, 2001. *Field Archaeology – An Introduction*. London: UCL Press.

Gamble, C, 2001. *Archaeology – The Basics*. London: Routledge.

Graves-Brown, P, Harrison, R & Piccini, A, 2013. *The Oxford Handbook of The Archaeology of the Contemporary World.* Oxford: Oxford University Press.

Greene, K, & Moore, T, 2010, 5th Edition. *Archaeology – An Introduction*. London: Routledge.

Hester, TR, Shafer, HJ, & Feder, KL, 1997, 7th Edition. *Field Methods in Archaeology*. Mountain View (CA): Mayfield Publishing Company.

Hicks, D, & Beaudry, MC, 2006. *The Cambridge Companion to Historical Archaeology*. Cambridge: Cambridge University Press.

Hodder, I, 1999. *The Archaeological Process – An Introduction.* Oxford: Blackwell.

Hommon, RJ, 2013. *The Ancient Hawaiian State.* Oxford: Oxford University Press.

Johnson, M, 1999. *Archaeological Theory – An Introduction.* Oxford: Blackwell.

Lee, RB, & DeVore, I, eds., 1968. *Man The Hunter.* Hawthorne, N.Y.: Aldine Publishing.

Liu L & Chen, X, 2003. *State formation in early China.* London: Duckworth.

McIntosh, SK, ed., 1999, *Beyond Chiefdoms: Pathways to complexity in Africa.* Cambridge: Cambridge University Press.

Parker Pearson, M, 2011. *Stonehenge: A new understanding.* New York: Experiment Publishing.

Pauketat, TR, 2007. *Chiefdoms and other archaeological Delusions.* Maryland: Rowman & Littlefield.

Renfrew, C, & Bahn, P, 2012, 6th Edition. *Archaeology – Theories, Methods and Practice.* London: Thames & Hudson.

Scarre, C, ed. 2005. *The Human Past – World Prehistory and the Development of Human Societies.* London: Thames & Hudson.

Tarlow, S, & Nilsson Stutz, L, eds. 2013. *The Oxford Handbook of the Archaeology of Death and Burial.* Oxford: Oxford University Press.

Acknowledgements

The author would like to thank the following colleagues whose 2014 New Year celebrations were brought to an abrupt end when tasked with reading through an earlier typescript of this book: David Kennedy, David Thompson, Andrew Fitzpatrick, David Rudkin and David Bird. Their comments were invaluable and the text immeasurably improved as a result. He also acknowledges his immense debt to innumerable scholars, past and present, a few of whose works appear in the bibliography. His English has been both improved and frequently simplified through the scrutiny of a close personal friend. Needless to say, any factual errors, misinterpretations, omissions, grammatical lapses and uses of clumsy and unnecessary jargon are entirely the result of either his ignorance, or stubbornness, or both. Never leastly but invariably lastly he wishes to thank his agent, Frances Kelly, whose talent for putting publisher and author together remains as bright as ever.

About the author

John Manley is an archaeologist who has excavated widely around the world, including sites in Italy, the Caribbean, Ethiopia, South Africa, Iran and Afghanistan, as well as western Europe and the UK. His most notable excavations have been at Fishbourne Roman Palace (Chichester, UK), the probable residence of a Client or Friendly King during the Roman annexation of southern Britain, and at Jerash (Roman *Gerasa*) in Jordan. He was CEO of the Sussex Archaeological Society, the largest county archaeological society in the UK, for 16 years. As well as holding a research degree in archaeology, he also has a strong interest in social anthropology, and holds a PhD in that field, applying the insights of anthropology to Roman archaeology. He is the author of numerous articles and several books, including: *Atlas of Prehistoric Britain* 1989; *The Atlas of Past Worlds* Cassell 1993; *The Roman Invasion of Britain* Tempus 2001; *The Archaeology of Fishbourne and Chichester* Lewes, 2008; *An Introduction to the Archaeology of the South Downs National Park*, Lewes 2012; *South Downs National Park – Archaeological Walking Guide* The History Press 2013; and *The Romans* in the *All That Matters* series, Hodder, 2013. He is currently the Honorary Research Fellow of the Sussex Archaeological Society.

Index

ALL THAT MATTERS: ARCHAEOLOGY

Index